D1230267

ARNOLD SCHÖNBERG

Schlosser and Wenisch, Prague

ARNOLD SCHÖNBERG

ARNOLD SCHÖNBERG

BY

EGON WELLESZ

Translated by W. H. KERRIDGE

*" The laws of Nature manifested in
a man of genius are but the laws
of the men of the future."*
ARNOLD SCHÖNBERG
(*Harmonielehre*)**.**

Select Bibliographies Reprint Series

BOOKS FOR LIBRARIES PRESS
FREEPORT, NEW YORK

First Published 1925
Reprinted 1969

STANDARD BOOK NUMBER:
8369-5059-3

LIBRARY OF CONGRESS CATALOG CARD NUMBER:
75-94286

PRINTED IN THE UNITED STATES OF AMERICA

927.8
W45
c.1.

Books For Libraries

9 SP

11 Feb 71

EDITOR'S PREFACE

DR. EGON WELLESZ, himself a composer of eminence, has here given us a biography and a study of the works of his master, who is not only one of the outstanding musical personalities of the present time, but also one of the most arresting figures in all music.

Hitherto, the chief source of information regarding Arnold Schönberg has been Dr. Wellesz's small book, first published in Vienna in 1921. At my request the author has revised this book, and in the process of revision has added so extensively to it that the present study of the composer is practically a new work.

I have acted on the author's suggestion that I should add some additional information on the compositions belonging to the 1920–24 period.

A. E.-H.

38307

CONTENTS

ARNOLD SCHÖNBERG

INTRODUCTION

In an age when whatever is said and written about art and artists has such a wide interest, it seems hardly necessary to justify, as it were, the motive for considering the creative activity of one of the leading musicians of the day. For every artist of note, even if he be not among the very great—the English speak of "minor poets" in literature—is nowadays the subject of biography and study.

But this very circumstance makes it difficult for me to write about a personality of such unusual calibre, and to act as intermediary between him and the public. In preparing this study, the chief object of which is to make Arnold Schönberg and his work better known to a wider circle, I feel the heavy responsibility and the difficulty of my undertaking, which is none other than to give a comprehensive and clear conception of a personality whose creative powers are still active and in process of transformation. Therefore I think it necessary to preface a few words that shall define my personal attitude to the problem I have undertaken.

It seems to me that only when one has a clear idea of technique and form, and follows the laws of construction, searching for what is indispensable and noting all deviations from accepted tradition, can advantage be derived from speaking on matters of art, instead of letting them simply exercise the immediate

I

appeal of their power. For such a method, which makes
a purely æsthetic explanation superfluous, brings us
nearer to the essentials of works of art, and removes
everything that could hinder the consideration of the
individual nature of that with which each art alone
is concerned.

Beyond this limit, however, words are of no avail,
and one reaches the unfathomable in the psychical
relation existing between a man who has produced
something from within him and one who feels the work
thus produced to be part of his own personal experience.
But the want of cohesion in our art-life, the result of
perpetually changing impressions that force themselves
upon us, has become so great that the public cannot
forgo, or believes it cannot forgo, the advice of those
whom it regards as guides in the flux of appearances.
For they can point out what is significant, or single
out works of art which strike them for some reason or
other as being of chief importance. They are, as it were,
receptacles in which are collected the thoughts and
tendencies of the period; or are like the lightning that
illuminates the darkness and destroys the forms of
the past.

To be the intermediary between the artist, his work,
and the public demands, above all, tact and a feeling of
detachment. However much enthusiasm he may have
for his task, and however important his subject may be,
the interpreter should never descend to the uttering of
panegyrics, nor in his praises adopt a tone that might
rouse the suspicion of those—by no means the least
worthy among such as occupy themselves with art—
who are reserved and distrustful towards every new
impression.

Still more important is the sense of perspective. The inability of many writers to keep at a proper distance from their subject is responsible for the fact that, among the general public, the right appreciation of uncommon men is so often lacking. At first, until such men have "arrived," people regard them with suspicion; later, when they have "arrived," people are prone to overwhelm them with exaggerated esteem. Through both attitudes, aloofness as well as over-esteem, there arises a gulf between artist and public. The lack of a natural position in society forces the artist against his will to live in isolation.

Our attitude towards a man of outstanding personality should be one of confidence, even if we do not at once understand all he does, since we allow to a man of genius unusual modes of expressing his thoughts. Just as we suffer what is unusual or estranging in the manners of one whom we esteem, because we assume that he will instinctively find the right way, so we put our faith in an artist of whose significance we may become aware only at rare moments, even if the greater part of the way he takes should strike us as being both strange and perplexing.

It often happens that men who have received little education, and are not burdened with the traditions of the past, more easily acquire confidence than such as have to struggle to overcome prejudices arising from tradition. And this may be the reason why the Germans, who can look back on a continuous and great musical past, find it generally more difficult to approach a novelty than nations that have just begun to develop an intensive musical life. This fact probably explains how it is that Schönberg first found recognition abroad

—in Holland, England, and Russia in particular. Nor is this recognition based on a real penetration into his work, such as we meet with in the deep understanding displayed by a small circle in Vienna, Prague and Berlin. It is rather the consequence of a vague feeling that there has arisen an artist of great force whose expressive qualities penetrate to our inmost being, and to whom we must pay deep respect.

.   .   .   .   .

From the foregoing remarks it will be possible to discover what has been my aim in giving an account of Schönberg's creative activity. It has been to show from what sources he has drawn in the course of his development; how his personality has gradually expressed itself, and how he has attained complete mastery of his work with the means handed down from the past, though infinitely widened; furthermore, how he, completely dominating those means, has discarded all that was merely traditional, and, listening only to the voice within him, has thus found his way into a new world of music, the wonderful extent of which only few as yet have recognised along with him.

But an ideal presentation of his work could not be wholly realised. For within the narrow limits of this book, prescribed by both time and circumstance, it is impossible to combine an exhaustive analysis of the works together with the necessary musical examples. Moreover, in preparing this book, I had to bear in mind that I was not only addressing myself to the professional musician, but also attempting to bring the amateur, from whom one cannot expect a knowledge based on musical training, into closer acquaintance with this much-discussed and highly problematic personality.

I was therefore obliged to strike a middle course, by doing which, however, I hope I have not had to make too many concessions. I have also sought to give a general survey of Schönberg in all his manifestations, and one can only partly do him justice if one considers his musical work alone. For his activity as a teacher occupies a large and essential part of his life, and bound up with that are his labours in the field of musical theory, the first systematic presentation of which is to be found in his *Harmonielehre* (*Manual of Harmony*).

In addition must be reckoned Schönberg's activity as poet and essayist. This began after the definite change in his musical style, and reached its culminating point in the words to *The Lucky Hand* and the oratorio *Jacob's Ladder*—the latter a work of great poetic power, the music of which is not yet complete. Though fully conscious of the difficulties and the inevitable imperfections that the task involved, I decided to write on Schönberg, because I judged that the time had come at least to make the first step towards a comprehensive exposition of the personality and creative work of an artist who is generally regarded as one of the leaders in the new movement in music, and whose influence on the younger generation has already made itself felt on every side.

This first attempt had of necessity to come from one who was not a stranger to the spiritual atmosphere in which Schönberg lived and worked. Without being able to number myself among the narrow circle of friends and pupils who had lived in closest contact with him—as, for instance, Anton von Webern and Alban Berg—I nevertheless enjoyed instruction in theory from him at a time most important for the intellectual and spiritual development of a young musician; and I received impressions that were decisive for my future. Later on, too, when outward circumstances and actual separation prevented personal intercourse, I did not cease to occupy myself with his works and analyse them. More than fifteen years ago I was quite convinced of the enormous significance of the artist who was at that time all but unknown, and decried by most native composers as being amateurish and even quite mad. It was also quite clear to me that his style was the expression of his own real nature, and the highest achievement of his personality. His example taught, moreover, that one should not simply take over the achievements of another, but persist in following the laws of one's own style and personality to the utmost limits. For I have always recognised that the right relation between pupil and teacher lies, not in the pupil's learning to become like his teacher, but in his being led by him to the development of his own innate powers. This much concerning my own artistic relations with Schönberg I feel it my duty to say.

I was present at the first performance of the two quartets, the *Gurre-Lieder*, the *Chamber-Symphony*, most of the songs, and also *Pierrot Lunaire*, and witnessed the tragedy of persistent attack on every new work that appeared. I saw also the disappointment of the composer and his circle of friends, which was quite small at first, but soon increased. They never could explain the fanatical antagonism of the critics and of a section of the audience towards Schönberg's music. They thought the seriousness and forceful expression of his music were sufficiently compelling at least to command respect, when on the contrary it met with ill-considered and malicious rejection. For how few there are that are capable of recognising the essential nature of a new phenomenon; how few that really know of its significance, or have a sure feeling for the true measure of a composition beyond the elementary problems of harmony and counterpoint; how few know when the driving power of a motive is at an end, when the melodic line should rise and when it should fall, and can feel where contrast is necessary in order to preserve the relative proportion of the whole!

In wider circles and among the younger generation now growing up, no idea can be formed of the attacks to which Schönberg was subjected, and of the suffering he had to endure. Nevertheless, I will not say too much of these things, the outcome of slow apprehension, lest I sink below the standard I have set and give this work a more or less local character—an attitude that may disappoint a number who may have expected a piece of propaganda in favour of "modern" music. I shall have to refer to these matters only in so far as they throw light on the difficulties with which Schönberg had to contend, and in order to explain his isolation from the outer world, to which he was obliged to have recourse, so that he might not be irritated into fruitless discussion with men who had nothing to give him.

It seems to me to be absolutely necessary to make a thorough study of Schönberg's early works if one would proceed to a full understanding of his compositions, and not to concern oneself solely with the later works, on which his reputation in England, France, and America is based. I am to some extent distrustful of people who know only *Pierrot Lunaire*, and admire Schönberg on the strength of this one work, without troubling to know his other compositions. Such an admiration seeks out from the treasures of a composer of genius the particular work that may have a certain effect on even an unpractised hearer, without considering that *Pierrot Lunaire* represents only a single link in a chain of which all the other links are of equal value. Schönberg's youthful works appeared just at a time when artists lived in the comfortable possession of all the equipment at their disposal. They regarded as a disturbing factor all that was bold, austere, or unusual; and they sought with all the means in their power to stifle it. Nowadays, when it is considered good form to be revolutionary, and when Schönberg has opened up a way for a new development in music, it is so easy to forget what had been accomplished between 1900 and 1910, and how much the present young generation owes to the pioneers.

Those who expect a "biography" of Schönberg will not be satisfied. Any such attempt seemed to me to be premature; moreover, it is quite unnecessary. One will get to know Schönberg much better through his works than through all that could be said or written about him. The outward circumstances of his life will be taken into account only in so far as they are necessary for fixing the dates of the origin of his works. In order to fix these I have gone through, with Schönberg himself, the first indications made in the original MSS., the most important source of which were three large books of sketches which he drew upon between 1904 and 1911. For valuable disclosures, especially concerning the first period of creative work, I am indebted to Anton Webern, who in a volume entitled *Arnold Schönberg* [1] has

---

[1] R. Piper & Co., Munich, 1912.

written an excellent essay on Schönberg's music. More-over I consulted Anton Berg's guides to the *Gurre-Lieder,* the *Chamber - Symphony* and *Pelleas und Melisande,* which in many respects may be regarded also as a direct source.

Naturally, I have not made use of the numerous essays written on Schönberg and some of his works, for the simple reason that I did not wish to give a mere compilation of other people's ideas on the subject. On the other hand, I have endeavoured to portray Schön-berg and his music as they strike me. If I succeed in giving outward expression to the inner life of Schön-berg, the problem I have set myself will be solved.

THE NEW PATH

I believe that art comes not of ability but of necessity. The practical artist *can* do something. What is innate within him he can develop, and if he only *wills* he *can*. What he *wills*—whether good or bad, shallow or profound, modern or antiquated—he *can*. But, above all, the artist *must*. He cannot influence what he produces; it depends not on his own will. But since necessity drives him, he can produce. He can even acquire what is not innate—manual skill, mastery of form, virtuosity. But such qualities are his own, not those of others. Genius, in other words, learns only from itself; talent chiefly from others. Genius learns from nature, from its own nature; talent learns from art.

IN these phrases, which form the introduction to a small essay — *Problems of the Teaching of Art* — written by Schönberg in 1911, are to be found the key to his creative activity. He became a musician in spite of everything.

There are musicians who, from their youth onwards, have been carefully prepared for their profession and ultimate aim in life, or have soon contrived to acquire a musical education. With Schönberg it was quite different; the thought of becoming a musician was far from his intention. Some inner compulsion gradually attracted him to music, and caused him to seek and find for himself all the necessary steps in musical education and advancement. And this "ability developed by compulsion from within" made him firm enough to trust to the voice of his inner being, and to write what he had to write, without concern for the creative activity of his contemporaries.

.   .   .   .   .

Arnold Schönberg was born in Vienna, on September 13th, 1874. His father, a merchant, died when the boy was sixteen years old. Through the early death of his father, Schönberg grew up in needy circumstances. When about the age of eight, he entered the Realschule, and learnt the violin. He composed short violin duets for his lessons; these were his first compositions. Later on he played chamber-music in a group formed of young people, such being a common practice among schoolfellows in Vienna. For these occasions he composed several trios. Thus he had a good opportunity of hearing his compositions and testing how they sounded. Later on, he taught himself the 'cello and wrote a string quartet.

It is interesting to observe how this youthful love of chamber-music became the guiding principle for all that he wrote. In the case of most young musicians of his generation, the decision to become a composer was due to the hearing of a music-drama by Wagner, or a symphony by Beethoven, and this would lead to a haphazard way of making music, forgetful of the necessity of acquiring skill and education. Schönberg, however, always remained true to the chamber-music style, even in his big orchestral works. He seeks to give each voice its own melodic outline, and he is able to express himself best whenever he can build on the polyphony of the string quartet.

The continued occupation with music nurtured his resolve to become a musician. He left the Realschule after reaching the sixth class, and worked entirely by himself for several years without any help and supervision from outside. A musician, to whom he showed several compositions in order to obtain his criticism, advised him to lay them before Alexander von Zemlinsky, who was held in high esteem by the young musicians of the time.

The meeting proved to be of decisive importance for Schönberg's future. Zemlinsky recognised the talent displayed in the works before him, and declared himself ready to give Schönberg instruction in counterpoint. Thus for many months, so long as his time permitted, he gave him regular instruction—the only instruction Schönberg ever got. The two met a good deal outside their work, and Schönberg played the 'cello in the orchestral society, Polyhymnia, which Zemlinsky conducted.

Through this association with Zemlinsky, which soon led to close friendship, Schönberg, who had hitherto held himself aloof from musical circles, came into the society of young musicians who used to meet in a café as is the custom in Vienna. At first it was the Café Landtmann opposite the Burgtheater; later, however, the Café Griensteidl, where all the young *intelligentsia* foregathered. A glowing enthusiasm for Wagner animated this circle—for *Tristan* in particular, whose style, orchestration and part-writing became the subject of serious discussion.

In the summer of 1897, Schönberg remained in Vienna in order to make the pianoforte arrangement of Zemlinsky's opera, *Sarema*, which was produced at the Munich Opera House. During this time he wrote a quartet which he showed to Zemlinsky. There was a good deal in the first and second movements that needed

revision; so Schönberg decided to re-write the first
movement and compose another in place of the second.
The last movement underwent considerable alteration,
but the third remained as it was. In its new form it received the approbation of his friend and counsellor, and
as such it was given in the concert-season 1897–98 by a
quartet specially formed for the purpose, the Wiener
Tonkünstler Verein; and in the following year, during
the season 1898–1899, it was repeated by the Pfitzner
Quartet.

This was the first public performance of a work by
Schönberg, and it met with great approval, since it was
conceived on traditional lines; but it already embodied
the great melodic warmth that the works of Schönberg's
youth so markedly show. This quartet was also his
"'prentice work"; henceforward he was to be master
of his own tools, and he began to find the mode of
expression which was adequate to himself.

The outcome of the first attempt to write a symphonic
poem, which was begun just after the quartet, remained
a fragment. After that, a full period of song-composition
set in, of which only a part was incorporated in the song
albums, Ops. 1 and 2. Already the first of these songs,
the two comprised in Op. 1, set to poems by Karl von
Lentzow, and *Freihold*, No. 6 of Op. 3 (composed at
this time), which Schönberg dedicated to his teacher
and friend, Alex. von Zemlinsky, showed him to be at
the full height of technical mastery. They were sung
for the first time in December 1900, by the Viennese
singing-master, Prof. Gärtner, at his song-recital, Zemlinsky playing the rich and unusually polyphonic accompaniment. When the performance was over, there was
a mild "scene" in the hall. "And from that time," said

Schönberg with a smile one day when he was telling me about it, "the scandal has never ceased."

In the late summer of 1899, Schönberg was again with Zemlinsky in Payerbach. There he composed, within a period of three weeks in September, the string sextet, Op. 4, *Verklärte Nacht*. It was based on a poem by Richard Dehmel. This poem, which now forms the introduction in *Romanes in Romanzen, i.e. Zwei Menschen*, at that time appeared in the first edition of the volume *Weib und Welt*.

The string sextet represents the first attempt (apart from Smetana's *Aus meinem Leben* quartet, which was entirely classical in construction) to apply to chamber-music the form hitherto confined exclusively to the large orchestra.

In March 1900, Schönberg began in Vienna the composition of a work on a larger scale than anything he had hitherto attempted—the choral work *Gurre-Lieder*. He was at the time conductor of several choral societies for working-men—one in Stockerau, near Vienna, a second in Meidling, and a third in Mödling. One spring night, after a convivial party, he made an excursion with the Mödlinger Gesangsverein (Choral Society) to the Anninger, a mountain in the neighbourhood. The stroll through the forest in the early morning mist, together with the sunrise, gave him his first inspiration for the third part of the melodrama, *The Summer Wind's Wild Chase*, and for the final chorus, *Behold the Sun*.

This work also, like everything that Schönberg has composed, was written in an incredibly short space of time. Already by the early part of 1900, the first, second, and the beginning of the third part had been finished. Then material anxieties forced him to interrupt his

composition, and to devote the whole of his time and
energy to the orchestration of operettas. One need be
no sentimentalist to find it intolerable that a work like
the *Gurre-Lieder* should have to be held up for a whole
year in order that the composer might earn a small
pittance by helping operetta-composers to convert their
wares into hard cash.

It was not until the March of 1901 that Schönberg
could resume the composition of the *Gurre-Lieder*, and
finish the third part, which was already in sketch form.
Schönberg had conceived for the performance an
orchestral and choral apparatus that would exceed all
that had been known hitherto. He ordered from the
Viennese printers, Waldheim-Eberle, some manuscript
paper (with forty-eight staves) in double the size known
until then. When this paper was produced in August,
he set about the orchestration at once. It is not superfluous to mention this, because an interest in technical
improvements for actual performance is highly characteristic of him. At the present time Schönberg is in
negotiation with the same firm for a re-arrangement
of staves, in order that the notes may be seen to better
advantage. For years he was engaged on attempts to set
up a music typewriter. In the printing of his works he
has carried out many important innovations; schemes
for the simplification of the full score will receive special
mention later.

About this time he married his friend's sister,
Mathilde von Zemlinsky, and went with her in 1901
to Berlin, where he hoped to find a better livelihood.
There at first he was engaged for a short time as conductor of Wolzogen's Buntes Theatre; he had to
conduct *Überbrettllieder*, and he composed one with

trumpet obbligato, which, as may well be imagined, proved to be too difficult, and had only one performance.

In Berlin, about the middle of 1902, Schönberg again took up the orchestration of the *Gurre-Lieder*, but soon he had to drop this on account of the orchestration of some operettas that he had undertaken. Once more, in the following year, he attempted to finish the work but he came to a standstill in the middle of the second part. The impossibility òf producing it took from him the power to accomplish the huge task he had set himself. In the first edition of the score, which is a photographic reproduction of his own handwriting, one can see the exact place where his work was interrupted.

For seven years, work on the *Gurre-Lieder* was held up. Only a few knew of the work and spoke of the wonders of orchestration and daring devices that nobody up to that time had attempted. Richard Strauss, to whom Schönberg showed the first part of the *Gurre-Lieder*, procured him the Liszt stipendium and a position as teacher of composition at the Stern Conservatoire. It was not until 1910 that Schönberg again took up the orchestration. He proceeded with it up to the final chorus, and finished the work in Zehlendorf near Berlin in 1911.

The composition of the *Gurre-Lieder* is therefore to be placed between March 1900 and April 1901. No part was subsequently added, as has often been asserted; but the whole work, with the exception of a few bars, took shape during this time. A letter from Schönberg to Alban Berg, which the latter inserted in his guide to the *Gurre-Lieder*, settles the matter. I quote the conclusion of this letter, because it contains a number of remarks that are significant of Schönberg generally:

The whole composition was thus finished, I should say,
in April or May 1901. Only the final chorus was still in
rough sketches, though in that, needless to say, the most
important voice-parts and the whole form were already
present. Indications of the orchestration were, in the
original composition, not very numerous. I did not note
them down at the time, because the tone-colour intended
was more or less obvious. But, apart from this fact, one
must see that the part orchestrated in 1910–11 is quite
different in style from the first and second parts. I had no
intention of concealing the fact; on the contrary, it is self-
evident that my orchestration of ten years later would
be different.

In finishing off the score I re-wrote only a few passages.
They were mostly groups of eight to twenty bars, especially
e.g. in the piece *Klaus the Fool* and in the final chorus. Everything else, even a good deal that I would willingly have had
otherwise, remained as it was at first. I could never have
found the style again, and even a half-practised connoisseur
would have discovered the four or five corrected passages.
These corrections cost me more trouble than the writing
of the whole composition at the time.

The first performance of the *Gurre-Lieder* was given on
February 23rd, 1913, by the Philharmonic Choir, Franz
Schreker conducting, in the large hall of the Musikverein in Vienna. It brought Schönberg his first great
success; and yet this success came too late. One must
remember that a work of art is not something absolute,
existing by and for itself, but something dependent on
the conditions of its reception. Much depends on the
point of time when the work first comes into contact
with the outer world. How important it would have been
for Schönberg if he could have finished the orchestration ten years earlier, and could then have brought the
work into publicity! One has only to think of the works
produced about the year 1900 to realise how novel and

strong the *Gurre-Lieder* would have seemed by comparison. At that time they marked the culminating point in his achievement. Later on he struck out beyond them; and one can understand that, at the time of the most bitter hostility to his works, he referred to the *Gurre-Lieder* as to something remote.[1]

Another big orchestral work had its origin in Berlin, namely the symphonic poem *Pelleas und Melisande*, Op. 5, after the drama by Maurice Maeterlinck. It was composed in 1902 and completed in 1903 up to the scene in the vaults under the castle, which is orchestrated with a mysterious glissando in the trombones.

In July of this year, Schönberg returned to Vienna and took up his abode in the same house as Zemlinsky. He spent the summer in Payerbach, where he temporarily took up the orchestration of the *Gurre-Lieder*, which, however, he soon dropped again. This period covers the composition of a number of songs and sketches for a choral work, and a string quartet which may be regarded as the predecessor of the D minor, Op. 7. In the autumn of this year, Schönberg began his activity as a teacher. Several classes were formed in the school buildings of Frau Dr. Schwarzwald. Schönberg taught harmony and counterpoint, Zemlinsky form and orches-

---

[1] Mr. Ernest Newman, writing of the *Gurre-Lieder* in the London *Musical Times* of Jan. 1914, says: "One's first feelings after a thorough study of the score are regret that this work should have remained in manuscript for thirteen years, and amazement that it should have been written by a young man of twenty-six. Its general idiom, even to-day, is more advanced than that of any contemporary German music; yet it was written three years before the *Symphonia Domestica*, and six years before *Salome*. It is quite evident, then, that Schönberg's style is one wholly native to him. It could not have been developed, say, out of Strauss or any other composer of our time, for there is simply nothing in Strauss out of which Schönberg's rich harmonic language could have been evolved."

tration, and Dr. Elsa Bienenfeld the history of music. In the Ansorge Verein (Association), songs of Schönberg were sung and the Rosé Quartet performed the sextet in the Vienna Tonkünstlerverein (Musicians' Association of Vienna), and also in one of their own concerts. At that time the first meeting with Gustav Mahler, who was then director of the Court Opera, took place at the rehearsals, which were held in the practice-rooms of the Opera House. Arnold Rosé had drawn Mahler's attention to the sextet. Mahler came to the rehearsal and was strongly impressed, and from that time onwards, Schönberg found in him a very willing and helpful friend and promoter.

In this year a change in Schönberg's style began to take place, and there began the period in which Schönberg became master of the strict form that went back to the classics. Already the *Six Songs with Orchestra*, which appeared as Op. 8, show an astonishingly firm construction. In the summer of 1904 Schönberg began, in Mödling, the *D minor String Quartet*, Op. 7, which he finished in the summer of 1905 in Gmunden on the Traumsee.

For a penetrative glimpse into the psychology of Schönberg's creative activity the books of sketches, of which he made exclusive use in the period of the first and second string quartet, the chamber-music, and the songs and sketches which fall into this period, are of the greatest importance. Nobody who has glanced at them will be able to say that Schönberg's music is "manufactured" or intellectual. Nor is it to be described in terms often employed by people who are afraid of admitting the superiority of his exuberant imagination. Every one of his thematic ideas is invented simultaneously with its counterparts. Whereas others have difficulty in combining the themes into a rich texture of several voices and of developing them adequately, Schönberg, on the other hand, has to apply a good deal of energy in stemming the spontaneous fullness of his ideas. And just as the simultaneity of the several thematic ideas must be transformed into a succession, so it is with the form in general. Seldom does Schönberg occupy himself with one work alone. Everywhere one finds interspersed between the several groups of quartets, songs or sketches of other chamber-music works that had remained unfinished although they had gone a considerable way in their development.

Schönberg's reputation as a teacher had much increased among the younger generation after the success of his winter-course 1903–4; especially with the group of music-historians then working at the Institute for Musical History of the University. Through the director of the Institute, Guido Adler, a friend of Gustav Mahler, we were admitted to the rehearsals of the latter's symphonies. We were interested in all that was new and out of the ordinary, and all of us had a strong dislike of the cut-and-dried instruction given us at the Conservatoire at that time. It was less the method that disturbed than the feeling that the teachers incessantly criticised all that seemed to us to be great and important. Of the pupils who grouped themselves around Schönberg at that time, several have remained in close contact with him throughout; among these are Anton von Webern, Alban Berg, Heinrich Jalowetz, and Erwin Stein.

· · · · ·

The conservative spirit, which never allowed any-

thing new to appear in the musical life of Vienna, forced
the young composers of the new school to continue in
the Association of Creative Musicians (Vereinigung
schaffender Tonkünstler). It included Zemlinsky, Schönberg, J. v. Wöss, Posa, Karl Weigl and Rudolf Hoff-
mann, and Gustav Mahler was elected honorary president. This association remained in activity only during
the winter, 1904–5, but a series of important works was
performed for the first time under its auspices—namely,
Mahler's *Kindertotenlieder* and songs from *Des Knaben
Wunderhorn*, the *Sinfonia Domestica* of Richard Strauss;
and in a concert in January 1905, the *Dionysische Phan-
tasie* of Siegmund v. Hausegger, *Seejungfrau* by Zemlinsky, and *Pelleas und Melisande* by Schönberg, who
conducted it himself.

I still remember perfectly well how difficult it was
to get a grasp of this latter work, and that Mahler
himself had no easy task, in reading the score, to get a
lucid idea of the part-writing. One must bear in mind,
of course, that the orchestra that produced it was unaccustomed to performing new works and played it
with much uncertainty, so that the resulting cool attitude
of the critics and bewilderment of the public were not
to be wondered at.

Nowadays one reads and hears it said by many people
—and indeed by those very people who at the beginning
poured contempt and even scorn upon it as being
utterly incomprehensible—that it is not so modern as
one would expect of a work by Schönberg; they, therefore, affect to be disappointed because they are now
obliged to confess, after time has put this work in its
proper perspective, how hastily and superficially they
had criticised at the time; how, with the rather cheap

objection that the work was Wagnerian in style, they diverted attention from what is essential, the luxurious wealth of intention, the noble conception of the themes, the astonishing art of the form and orchestration, and concentrated on one or two details appertaining to certain limitations in the music of the time, which none helped to overcome more than Schönberg himself.

After Schönberg had completed the quartet in the spring and summer of 1905, he began to compose a male chorus, *Georg von Frundsberg*, which was to form a second part to the song Op. 3, No. 1 from *Des Knaben Wunderhorn*, but it remained unfinished. Also there is a portion of a quintet which was begun in the autumn. Moreover, the *Eight Songs*, Op. 6, originated at this time: *Traumleben* by Julius Hart, *Alles* by Richard Dehmel, *Der Wanderer* by Friedrich Nietzsche, *Am Wegrand* by John Henry Mackay (composed on Oct. 18th, 1905), *Lockung* by Kurt Aram (composed on Oct. 26th), and *Mädchenlied* by Paul Reiner (composed on Oct. 28th). They were written in a white heat in the small hours of the morning, which were the only times Schönberg could spare from his teaching duties.

A prize competition promoted by the Berlin illustrated paper *Die Woche*, for the best composition of a Ballade, stimulated Schönberg to write the first of the two Ballades, *Jane Grey* and *Der verlorene Haufen*, in the spring of 1906. They are marked as Op. 12, and were not published till 1920. Schönberg did not get the prize.

Between some sketches for an opera after Gerhardt Hauptmann's *Und Pippa tanzt*, there appear, in the books of sketches, the first outlines of the *Chamber-Symphony* in E major, Op. 9, which was composed in the spring and summer of 1906 in Tegernsee. But simultaneously Schönberg began to work at a second Chamber-Symphony, the first theme of which was noted down on August 1st. This is quite a peculiar case, and it is remarkable to observe how his labours at these two compositions intertwine. Ultimately Schönberg gave up the idea of completing the second, although he had written more than half of it.

Strenuous activity as a teacher considerably limited his composing during the autumn and winter of this year. Only a chorus, *Friede auf Erden* (*Peace on Earth*), Op. 13, appeared; the text was the poem by C. F. Mayer, and the work was finished on March 9th, 1907. But the public was at last to become acquainted with Schönberg and his works. The Rosé Quartet had rehearsed the D minor quartet over forty times and ultimately gave it in the Bösendorfer Hall on February 5th, 1907. On this occasion arose the discussion, mentioned in Mahler's biography, between Schönberg himself and a man who stood up at the end of the performance and blew on a latchkey; the excitement of feeling for and against Schönberg was so great that it nearly gave rise to a scene in the concert-hall. This, as a matter of fact, did happen shortly after, when the Rosé Quartet, in conjunction with the Association of Wind Instruments of the Court Opera, performed the *Chamber-Symphony* in the large hall of the Music Association. The public did not trouble to wait for the end of the symphony, but interrupted the performance by banging seats, whistling, and by their ostentatious departure. In order to avoid further disturbances at performances, Schönberg, on the occasion of a second recital that took place in the spring of that year in the Ehrbar Hall, had cards printed bearing the notice that the possession of a card gave the right only to quiet listening, but to no expression of opinion whether by applause or by hissing. Frau Drill-Oridge and Herren Preuss and Moser, of the Opera House, sang songs out of Op. 2, 3, and 6, Zemlinsky accompanying on the piano. The success of this performance gave Schönberg much encouragement.

In the spring of 1907, Mahler, tired of opposition, left the opera and withdrew to Toblach, in order to be free to compose there, after he had signed a contract for America. Mahler's withdrawal from a leading position in the musical life of Vienna meant to Schönberg the loss of some very active help. Arnold Rosé and his fellow-players regarded it as their honourable duty to uphold Schönberg, and their unselfish devotion at a time when it was still a bold thing to appear in his favour, cannot be sufficiently appreciated. They also undertook to play the D minor quartet in June at the Thirty-third Musical Festival in Dresden, after it had been rejected in another quarter as being entirely unplayable.

In this year there began a new transformation of style in Schönberg's creative work, which, lasting up to the year 1909, led him to break away from bad tradition and speak in his own language. To this period of transition belong the *George Lieder* and the *Drei Klavierstücke*, Op. 11, in which the new style is already embodied.

The string quartet in F sharp minor was begun in Vienna on March 9th, 1907, and finished in Gmunden on September 1st. On the same day on which the quartet was begun, the chorus *Friede auf Erde*, which was written for a competition, was finished, and on that day, too, the first movement of the chorus, which was entirely instrumental and in strict style, was performed. The composition of the second Ballade, *Der verlorene Haufen*, also falls into the period, during which he was working at this quartet and at the beginning of the third, which, however, remained unfinished. The second Chamber-Symphony was also taken up again, only to be put on one side.

On December 17th, 1907, the song, *Ich darf nicht dankend an dir niedersinken* (*I may not in my gratitude kneel before thee*), Op. 14, No. 1, out of *Waller im Schnee*, by Stefan George, was begun; this was the first song in the new style and formed genetically a prologue to the second movement of the second string quartet, in which the voice appears. In gradual succession there appeared the *Fifteen Songs*, Op. 15, from Stefan George's *Book of the Hanging Gardens*.

Schönberg was again in Gmunden in the summer of 1908, and took up again the composition of the string quartet. The scherzo was finished on 21st July, and then the second movement with voice came into being. In between he still worked at the second Chamber-Symphony, sketches of which are to be found as early as 1911. Then the plan of finishing was finally given up. In the autumn appeared the last of the *George Lieder*.

Immediately after the completion of the F sharp minor quartet, Rosé began to rehearse it. The vocal part was undertaken by Frau Gutheil-Schoder of the Opera, who had already sung Schönberg's songs on many occasions. This performance, which took place in December in the Bösendorfer Hall, led to wild scenes. In the middle of a pause in the scherzo there was a burst of organised laughter. People whistled and hissed. Musicians of repute forgot themselves so far as to take part in this undignified behaviour, which was repeated in the third

c

and fourth movements. Whereupon the Ansorge Verein stepped in and brought about a repetition of the quartet before specially invited guests. It was preceded by the sextet, which was already known at the time, and which people were glad to hear as a set-off against the later work. Now for the first time one could get a complete and undisturbed impression.

At the beginning of the year 1909 appeared the *Drei Klavierstücke*, Op. 11, the first being No. 2, finished on February 22nd, the second No. 1, finished on March 19th, and finally the third. They were performed at a concert for the Verein für Kunst und Kultur (Association of Art and Culture) given by Frau Etta Werndorff, and were first played in public by Dr. Rudolf Reti. They were preceded by the first performance of the first part of the *Gurre-Lieder*, with pianoforte accompaniment, and also the *George Lieder*.

In order to render more intelligible the way that leads from the *Gurre-Lieder* to the *George Lieder* and to the *Klavierstücke*, Schönberg wrote the following preface, which appeared on the programme of that evening:

The *Gurre-Lieder* were written at the beginning of 1900, the *George Lieder* and the *Klavierstücke* in 1908. The interval that lies between these works explains perhaps the great difference in style that is obvious in them. The combining of such heterogeneous works in an evening's performance, since it expresses a certain definite idea, perhaps also needs some justification. In the *George Lieder* I have succeeded for the first time in approaching an ideal of expression and form that had hovered before me for some years. Hitherto I had not sufficient strength and sureness to realise that ideal. Now, however, that I have definitely started on my journey, I may confess to having broken off the bonds of a bygone æsthetic; and if I am striving towards a goal that seems to me to be certain, nevertheless I already feel the opposition that I shall have to overcome. I feel also with what heat even those of the feeblest temperament will reject my works, and I suspect that even those who have hitherto believed in me will not be willing to perceive the necessity of this development. Therefore it seems to me opportune to show, through the performance of the *Gurre-Lieder*, which found no friends eight years ago, but which to-day have many, that it is not lack of invention or of technical skill, nor of the knowledge of the other demands of contemporary æsthetics, that has urged me in this direction, but that I am following an inner compulsion that is stronger than education, and am obeying a law that is natural to me, and therefore stronger than my artistic training.

At this point it is necessary to mention that the artistic process of transformation, which forced Schönberg to listen to the voice within and obey it, was accompanied by a need for an increased power of expression, and this very need led him to give to his vision concrete form. With a perfectly astonishing talent he learnt the technique of painting, and in the time between 1907–10 he painted a large number of pictures. His pictures fall into two clearly defined groups, namely, portraits and nature studies on the one hand, and on the other "colour visions." Whatever one's attitude towards these may be, one is, nevertheless, amazed at the power and directness of the artistic will that is behind them. One feels that they *had* to be painted in order to dominate the exuberant fancy within.

As Schönberg acquired the mastery of the new musical technique, which he himself had created, the need to express himself in colour gradually disappeared and finally ceased altogether. An exhibition of his pictures in the autumn of 1910 at Heller's Art Gallery had the result that even people who had nothing to do with music, on the strength of the impression they gained from the exhibition, now believed they had the right to express an opinion on Schönberg the composer. Only a few felt the inner necessity that urged the solitary artist to express himself visually, and were thus able to penetrate more deeply into his music.

At the beginning of 1909, Schönberg embarked on the composition of the *Fünf Orchesterstücke*, Op. 16, the score of which he completed in the summer in Steinkirchen, near Amstetten. He then set about the composition of the monodrama *Erwartung* (*Expectation*), the text of which was by Marie Pappenheim, who received the idea from Schönberg. He wished in this way to portray how, in moments of fearful tension, the whole of one's life seems to flash again before one's eyes. The poetic outline was developed by the authoress of the text on the basis of the following idea. A woman goes through a wood by night seeking for her lover, but when she finds him he is dead. The fleeting thoughts that course through her mind during her anxious search, and on the discovery of the dead man find vent in accents rendered intense by misery, evoke music in which all the subtleties of feeling are expressed, from the utmost tenderness to outbursts of rage and pain.

Schönberg composed this dramatic work, the performance of which lasts about half an hour, in the period between August 27th and December 12th, 1909 — that is to say, in about fourteen days. Hence in this work one cannot speak of "manufactured music."

After the completion of *Erwartung*, Schönberg began to work at a second dramatic composition, the text of which he himself wrote. Just as in the case of *Erwartung* one must not regard it from the point of view of the traditional theatre, so in this new drama, *Die Glückliche Hand* (*The Lucky Hand*), one must exclude all that one associates with stage-production, and imagine a scene wherein the miraculous can happen without being caused by an external process, because all that happens comes from within. The first publication of this dramatic poem took place in a special Schönberg number of the Viennese musical journal, *Der Merker*, edited by R. Specht.

One is most likely to discover the lines on which this drama is written if one thinks of the chamber-plays of Strindberg, for whose works Schönberg had an extraordinary admiration. In this work is to be found an expressionist style long before this term had been adopted, the carrying out of which proceeded on a preconceived theory.

The composition of *The Lucky Hand*, to which Schönberg devoted himself immediately after the completion of the poem, proceeded, unlike *Erwartung*, slowly and in spurts. The score was not completed until November 18th, 1913. *Erwartung* had already been played by the pianist Eduard Steuermann to Count Seebach, Intendant of the Dresden Opera, and to the conductor, Schuch. The latter betrayed the greatest interest in the music, and Count Seebach was fascinated by the technical problems it involved from the point of view of the stage. On this occasion Schönberg laid before Schuch several pages of *The Lucky Hand*, and was advised by him to finish the work and perform both together. Thus encouraged, Schönberg began anew the composition of *The Lucky Hand* and finished it. Steuermann worked hard at the pianoforte edition of both dramatic works. The outbreak of the war prevented the performance that had been planned; also the piano editions came to a stop.

There was a good deal that prevented Schönberg from a rapid completion of this work, corresponding indeed to the natural rhythm of his creative activity. Outward circumstances, such as the moving into Ober-St. Veit, a suburb of Vienna, intensive work at painting, the resumption of the orchestration of the *Gurre-Lieder*, and the beginning of the writing of the *Harmony Manual*, all hindered it. This additional and many-sided work on the one hand, and on the other his living outside the city, resulted in Schönberg's spending the summer in Vienna. In the autumn he journeyed to Berlin, where, in October, Oskar Fried conducted a performance of *Pelleas und Melisande*; this was the first performance abroad of any orchestral work by Schönberg. After his return there was a performance of both quartets by Rosé, in connection with the exhibition of Schönberg's paintings in Heller's Art Gallery already mentioned, Frau Gutheil-Schoder singing the vocal part. On this occasion, Schönberg saw Gustav Mahler for the first time before his voyage to America, and he told him that he intended to dedicate the *Harmony Manual* to him. Mahler was delighted at this; but no one who saw him at the time had the least idea that he would be seen no more. In consequence the *Harmony Manual*, which Schönberg finished in 1911, has the following dedication:

This book is dedicated to the memory of Gustav Mahler. It was hoped that the dedication might give him some small joy while he still lived. It was intended thereby to do honour to his immortal compositions and to show that his work, at

which cultivated musicians in their superiority shrugged
their shoulders and which they even passed by with contempt, was revered by one who perhaps to some extent
understood it.

Gustav Mahler has had to forgo far greater joys than
that which the dedication of this book might have brought
him. This martyr, this saint, had to leave this earth before
he had so far advanced his work as to be able to hand it
over to his friends in all tranquillity.

I should have contented myself with offering him this
satisfaction: but now that he is dead it is my wish that my
book may bring me this esteem, that none may gainsay me
when I say, "Truly he was a great man."

Of the *Sechs kleine Klavierstücke*, Op. 19, composed
in the spring of 1911, the last came into being as the
result of the impression made on him by Mahler's
funeral. In the spring and summer, the orchestration
of the *Gurre-Lieder* continued along with his labours on
the *Harmonielehre*. Then in the summer, Schönberg
journeyed to Munich, and decided to withdraw from
Vienna and settle in Berlin. At the time, an attempt was
made to keep Schönberg in Vienna. He could have kept
up his courses on composition at the Association for
Music and the Plastic Arts without, however, holding
a regular position as a professor. This was not to
happen. The attacks in public and the interpellations
of a Member of Parliament made it seem advisable to
Schönberg to decline the offer made at that time by
the President of the Association.

He took up his abode in Zehlendorf, near Berlin, and
it was here that he completed the *Harmonielehre*, continued the composition of *The Lucky Hand*, and wrote
the music for Maurice Maeterlinck's poem *Herzgewächse*. This composition, Op. 20, for high soprano,

celesta, harmonium and harp, first appeared in the *Blaue Reiter*, edited by Kandinsky and Franz Marc.

In the autumn of 1911, Schönberg began a series of ten lectures on æsthetics and composition in the hall of the Stern Conservatoire of Music, and he made the acquaintance of the actress, Albertine Zehme, at whose suggestion he composed in melodramatic form a cycle consisting of three groups of seven songs from the poem *Pierrot Lunaire* by Albert Giraud in Otto Erich Hartleben's translation. This work was written in the spring and summer of 1912: the first, *Mondestrunken* (*Moonstruck*), on March 30th, and the last, *Die Kreuze* (*The Crosses*), on September 9th.

Already during the composition of *Pierrot Lunaire* Schönberg began preparations for its performance. Over forty rehearsals were held with Frau Zehme and the chamber orchestra, consisting of members of the Royal Orchestra, and with the pianist Eduard Steuermann, a pupil of Busoni.

In the autumn the first performance took place in Berlin, after which a tour was made of many towns in Germany. The tour was extended to Prague and Vienna, where a performance was given in the Bösendorfer Hall. In November, Schönberg was invited to Amsterdam to conduct *Pelleas und Melisande* with the Concertgebouw Orchestra. He had performed this work in February of the same year in Prague with the Philharmonic Orchestra, which for the first time this season was under the direction of Zemlinsky. The performance in Amsterdam, where the orchestra had been brought to a marvellous pitch of technical skill by Mengelberg, resulted in an enormous success which had a lasting effect, and which was to be of the highest importance for Schönberg. Immediately after this performance he was invited to St. Petersburg to conduct the work there.

When one compares the criticisms of the performances of this work both at home and abroad, one is astonished at the unstinted recognition with which Schönberg's appearance was received abroad in contrast with his reception in Germany and Austria. I was especially struck by a study of Schönberg's work by Ernst Pingoud, in the *Montagsblatt* of the *St. Petersburger Zeitung* of July 1 (14), 1913, in which the critic places side by side the compositions on the same theme by Debussy and Schönberg, and points out how Schönberg has raised his material from the particular to general. One can understand that Schönberg's friends, in view of the perpetual anxieties with which he had to fight, should have felt the desire to give him a visible proof of their devotion, and so the collection of essays and contributions, which was published in 1912 by R. Piper and Co. in Munich, was dedicated to him.

Nevertheless Schönberg was to experience a huge public success at this time in Vienna, in the first performance of the *Gurre-Lieder*. Franz Schreker, the conductor and artistic director of the Philharmonic Choir in Vienna, had taken it upon himself to help at last towards a "performance of the chief work of a very much discussed composer"—so ran a notice which was sent round in the spring of 1912. The performance, which involved an unusually large expense, took place on Sunday, February 23rd, 1913, in the large hall of the Music Association, under the direction of Franz Schreker. Frau Winternitz-Dorda sang *Tove*, Frau Marya Freund *The Forest Dove*, Herr Hans Nachod

Waldemar, Herr Boruttau *Klaus the Fool,* Herr Nosalewicz *The Peasant,* and the part of the speaker was delivered by Herr Gregori of the Burgtheater. Long and careful rehearsals in the presence of Schönberg preceded the performance. Unfortunately for Schönberg, the joy of this success in his native city was not to remain for long undisturbed.

In order to do something for his pupils Anton von Webern and Alban Berg, Schönberg decided to conduct an orchestral concert that was to be given under the auspices of the Akademischer Verband für Literatur und Musik (Academic Society for Literature and Music). It took place on March 31st in the large hall of the Musikverein, and included orchestral pieces by Webern, Schönberg's *Chamber-Symphony,* orchestral songs by Zemlinsky and Alban Berg, and the *Kindertotenlieder,* by Mahler. Apparently one section of the public had come with the intention of creating a scene, for one saw many people, including operetta-composers, who had held themselves aloof from performances of modern music. Even during Webern's orchestral pieces and Schönberg's *Chamber-Symphony* there arose an altercation between students, who were enthusiastically applauding, and certain people who sought to disturb the performance by shouts and hisses. When it came to the songs by Berg, however, the noise was so great that one could scarcely hear anything at all. In these circumstances, Schönberg wanted to discontinue his conducting, but he nevertheless yielded to persuasion; so he made a request, through the superintendent of the Academic Society, that at least the songs of Mahler might be received with the "fitting quiet and respect due to the composer."

As a result of this appeal, several people, who up to
that point had disturbed the concert in the most in-
considerate manner conceivable, apparently felt offended
and scenes followed which I will not attempt to describe.
The performance ended in a wild struggle in which
blows were exchanged. It found its echo in the law
courts, where a well-known operetta-composer, called
as a witness, said, "Well, I laughed myself, and why
shouldn't one laugh at what is obviously funny?" And
another, a practising doctor, declared that the effect of
the music was "for a certain section of the public, so
nerve-racking, and therefore so harmful for the nervous
system, that many who were present already showed
obvious signs of severe attacks of neurosis."

I do not mention this matter merely to give to a purely
local affair an importance it does not deserve—later
there were similar scenes in the performances of Schönberg's works, for instance, at the performance of the
Fünf Orchesterstücke in Paris in the spring of 1922—but
in order to make it clear that, in these circumstances,
Schönberg could not wish to expose himself to such
scenes. He became more reserved and more aloof from
the world than ever, and it was only with the utmost
difficulty that one could persuade him to allow his
works to be performed.

Nevertheless it was quite impossible to ignore so
important and distinguished a personality as Schönberg's. The work was there and began to attract interest
throughout the entire world. Oskar Fried conducted,
in Paris in July 1913, the "Song of the Forest Dove,"
from the *Gurre-Lieder*, with Marya Freund; and at a
Queen's Hall Promenade Concert, on September 3rd,
1912, Sir Henry Wood performed, for the first time, the

Five Orchestral Pieces. Schönberg was himself invited
to conduct a repetition of the work in February 1914.
From London, Schönberg travelled to Leipzig, where,
after sixteen rehearsals, he gave a performance of the
Gurre-Lieder. From there he went via Berlin for the
second time to Amsterdam, in order to perform the
Five Orchestral Pieces. In addition to this a performance
of *Pelleas und Melisande* was given in Mannheim.

The outbreak of the war put an end to the international activity which was just beginning. Schönberg
remained in Berlin, entirely given up to his teaching
work. During this time he conceived the plan of a large
oratorio in three parts, the first part of which was based
on a poem by Dehmel, whereas for the second and third
parts he himself wished to compose the text. The
beginning of the idea of such a work dates back to 1910.
At first he did not get beyond the preliminary sketches
for this work. Then there appeared in a short time the
Four Songs, Op. 22, for voice and orchestra, published
in a simplified student's conducting score. The first
of the songs, *Seraphita,* by Stefan George, was composed
as early as October 6th, 1913; the fourth, *Vorgefühl*
(Premonition), by Rainer Maria Rilke, appeared on
August 28th, 1914, the third on December 3rd, 1914,
and the second between December 30th, 1914, and January 1st, 1915. A short time after, on January 15th, the
poem of the second part of the oratorio, *Der Totentanz*
der Prinzipien, conceived as a scherzo, was written down.
Three days later, Schönberg began the poem for the
third part, *Die Jakobsleiter (Jacob's Ladder),* which,
interrupted again by his military service, was not
finished until July 1917. This part developed into a
self-contained whole to such an extent, that Schönberg

relinquished the original plan of a work in three parts
and let this poem appear as an independent oratorio.

As was the case with the *Testo* (*Witness*), and with
the passion-play, *The Evangelist*, so here throughout, the
work represents a chain of prayers of ascending degrees.
The leading figure is the Archangel Gabriel; it is he who
answers the crowd of the oppressed, the man who has
been bewitched, the rebel, the soldier, the monk, the
dying man; and it is he who points out the way for
their salvation.

The music to this poem remains a fragment owing to
the fact that Schönberg was on military service from
December 1915 to September 1916, and again from July
to October 1917. Immediately after the completion of
this poem he worked at the composition of the music
up to the very day of his second "calling-up." But
the enforced abandonment of this psychical excitement
and high intellectual activity so destroyed the con-
tinuity of the work that he never returned to the composition. He devoted himself entirely to teaching. In the
rooms of the Black Forest Schools, which were placed at
his disposal for this purpose, he opened a Seminary for
Composition, with the intention, instead of limiting the
instruction to hourly lessons, of giving the pupils opportunities for coming into closer contact with their teacher.

In April 1918 he withdrew to Mödling, near Vienna,
and collected round him a wider circle of pupils. In
order to give the students, and also the wider public,
a practical introduction to contemporary music together
with theoretical instruction, the Verein für Müsicalische
Privataufführungen (Association for Private Musical
Performances) was founded, the president being Arnold
Schönberg himself. It opened its activities in the autumn

with regular weekly performances. In the early part
of the next year, the *Chamber-Symphony* was studied in
ten public rehearsals, without any actual public performance, in order that opportunity might be given for
people to get thoroughly acquainted with the artistic
construction of the composition. In the following year
Schönberg himself conducted it in Vienna, and there
performed, in choral setting, the two string quartets.

In the year 1920 the world again began to open out
to him. He conducted his works in Prague, Mannheim
and Amsterdam. In the latter place it was proposed
that he should give a course in musical theory. Nothing
came of the proposal, but Willem Mengelberg again
raised the matter when a short time later, on the occasion
of the Mahler Festival in May 1920, Schönberg returned
to Amsterdam, where he was also nominated President
of the newly formed International Mahler-Bund.

Schönberg decided to accept the invitation to Amsterdam for the autumn and winter 1920–21. On returning
to Vienna he immediately began with the rehearsals of
the *Gurre-Lieder*, which, as the chief feature of the
Vienna Music Festival, were performed with the augmented Philharmonic Orchestra under his direction on
June 12th and 13th, 1920, at the Opera House. A few
days before, *Pelleas und Melisande* was given with great
success by Zemlinsky.

In 1922 he issued a new and revised edition of his
Harmony Manual, without altering in any way the
original character of the work, which is quite orthodox.
In 1923 he produced a cycle of piano pieces, a piano
suite, a wind quintet and a *Serenade* for a septet of
instruments—clarinet, bass-clarinet, mandoline, guitar,
violin, viola and 'cello.

With the performance of the *Gurre - Lieder* in the
Vienna Opera House, to which musicians from America
and Holland had come, the most difficult stages for him,
and for the spreading abroad of his works, were overcome. He had, with the greatest effort and struggle, and
without any concessions of whatever kind, created a
position for himself through the power of his will and
the purity of his intention, which ultimately compelled
all, even those who were estranged by his works, to offer
him homage and respect. Those who demand that all
that is inexplicable in his works should be expressed in
words and brought nearer to them, forget that genius
does not conform to the times, but that the times must
conform to genius. Yet whoever has a penetrative knowledge of his work realises that all comes from one fount;
that stages which others, weaker than he, might need
are passed over, and the way, for which often whole
generations are necessary, is here traversed by a single
personality.

HIS TEACHING

SCHÖNBERG'S activities are so interwoven that one cannot mention him as a teacher without thinking of him as a conductor, nor as a conductor without thinking of his theoretical compositions. Here I will endeavour rather to give a description of Schönberg's general activities than to deal separately with his work as a teacher and a conductor.

Schönberg has a great talent for teaching; he is stimulating and effective. There is scarcely one of his many pupils who has not succumbed to the charm of his personality. An entire contrast to that of many instructors who regard their work merely as a means of obtaining a livelihood, Schönberg's life is full of thought for his pupils. Regardless of the rest of the world, he gives them freely of all that he has conceived, and draws from them whatever latent capability they may possess.

Those who might come to him for information on "modern" music, in particular those who wished to learn "modern" composition, would come to the wrong person. As in earlier days the great masters of handicrafts and art took pupils to live with them, that they might watch over them in the workshop or studio as they worked, so Schönberg gathers his pupils around him. He demonstrates to them the works of the great masters, from Bach to Brahms, discusses them and makes his pupils analyse them. He also urges his pupils to examine their own compositions and discover for themselves wherein lies any fault or clumsiness; he then points out better solutions—not one, but many—in order to show them clearly the abundant possibilities of realisation.

In a book dedicated to Schönberg, which contains many stories of his life, a pupil describes how he took to Schönberg a song that he himself particularly admired because of its extreme difficulty. Schönberg looked it through and then said, "Do you really mean this to be so complicated? Did your first idea contain this complicated form of accompaniment?" The student was surprised, and at a loss for an answer. He was considering one when Schönberg, who had already summed up the technique of the song, stuck to his point and asked further, "Have you not subsequently added this figure in order to deck out the harmonic structure, in the same way as façades are added to a building?" Thus Schönberg had probed to the bottom of the matter. The student admitted that the first idea had been purely harmonic, and that the plan of the accompaniment had been added later. "Then see that you keep your song to plain harmonies. It will appear simple, but will be the more genuine. What you have here is mere ornament. This is a three-part invention embellished with a voice part. Music, however, should not be adorned, but should be true. Wait patiently until an idea, which is immediately rhythmical, shall come to you. You will be surprised at the strength of impulse such an idea will bring with it. Look at Schubert's song *Auf dem Flusse*, and see how each successive movement leads on to the next. Nothing should come to you with difficulty. What you compose must be as natural to yourself as are your hands and

D

clothes. Until that happens, you should write nothing. The simpler ycur inspiration seems, so much the better will it be. Some other time bring me a work that you do not consider worthy to be shown me because it is too simple and lacking in finish. I will prove to you that it is more genuine than this. It is only with things that are organic to you, and therefore self-evident, that I can begin. When you find something you have written is very complicated, you should at once be doubtful of its genuineness."

This is no isolated case. It was so with all who studied under Schönberg, whether it was the filling-in of a part, or some artificial harmonisation, or a case of overloading the score. With an extraordinary keenness of observation he is immediately able to differentiate between the essential and the unessential, real feeling and affectation. Pupils, who have previously learned under other masters, will give up what they have only outwardly assimilated, and will, with double care, examine every idea that comes to them.

And this seems to me to be the essential thing. Schönberg demands that the simplest examples, and even the earliest harmony exercises, should be written at high tension. In this way he aims at welding together, as closely as possible, talent, inspiration, and technique, and proves that it is the idea itself that should exhibit all its latent possibilities of application and development. To him technique and invention grow together, an inseparable whole. On this account he thought it impossible for anyone to have a knowledge of technique but no power of invention. Either one has no technique, or one has inventive power as well. "He has not technique," he writes in the *Problemen des Kunstunterrichtes*

(*Problems of the Teaching of Art*), "who can just skil-
fully imitate something given; rather he is the slave
of technique—the technique of another. Whoever is
capable of perceiving aright, must realise that such
technique is fraudulent. Nothing really fits in properly;
it is merely put together with some skill. In such a case
nothing is exact, nor develops out of itself, nor holds
together; viewed from a distance, however, it seems genuine
enough. There is no technique without invention; but
invention must create its own technique."

In teaching, Schönberg proceeds by the opposite road
to that taken by most teachers. If we look through the
small *Modulation Manual* of Max Reger we find there
instructions for the art of passing, most simply and
quickly, from one key to another. But that is only one
way among many and gives the student no idea of the
multiplicity of solutions. Schönberg shows in all possible
ways, from the simplest to the remotest transition
through the various keys, that the pupil can go from the
nearest to the most remote and back without being
conscious of having left the original key. So these
exercises in modulation are already studies in the
construction of the smaller forms.

He gives no system, as does Riemann, by means of
which the most complicated structure may be reduced to
simple formulæ, but he teaches a craftsmanship instead.
The ideal hovering before him is to let the student watch
the process of composition, as in the case of painting.
Proceeding from this consideration, he projected the
plan of a *Seminar für Komposition* (Seminary for Composition), which he maintained from 1917–1920. The
prospectus, which was issued before the institution was
opened, gives a good idea of Schönberg's schemes and

of the principal aims he had in view. I cannot do better than quote word for word:

"One only learns perfectly that for which one has some natural gift. In such cases no specific pedagogic rules and regulations are necessary; the stimulus to imitate afforded by a prototype is sufficient; one learns for what purpose one is created without knowing how, and one learns just so much as is commensurate with one's natural capacity.

" Owing to the fact that the number of things to be learnt becomes ever greater, and the time at disposal for their acquirement becomes relatively less, it has become necessary to supplement a desultory manner of study with some systematic teaching. It is a matter for astonishment that many men can attain to a certain standard of 'instruction' in things for which they have very little capacity. It cannot, on the other hand, be denied that the results are generally very mediocre. Especially is this the case in the domain of art. Whereas formerly there were amateurs who could not be distinguished from artists, in so far as their ability was concerned, except for the fact that they did not regard their artistic activity as a means of livelihood—nowadays, on the other hand, there are all too many artists who may be distinguished from amateurs not so far as their ability is concerned, but rather from the fact that they regard their artistic abilities almost entirely as a means of livelihood; the efficient amateur has become relatively scarce.

" The chief cause of the phenomenon is pedagogism. It demands from both artist and amateur at once too much and too little: the end in view. Too little, since within the scope of the instruction set forth it gives

more than the student needs, and as a result he is spared
the trouble of producing from within that abundance of
powers which helps to enrich natural gifts; too much,
since it gives him, in the same way, less than he needs,
and in consequence his latent powers are crippled, and
he himself is prevented from becoming that specialist
which, to judge from his natural disposition, he might
have become. In art there is only one true teacher,
aptitude; and that has only one useful assistant, namely,
imitation."

In the seminary not only the usual subjects, harmony,
counterpoint, form, orchestration, which form part of
the curriculum in conservatoires, were taught, but also
evening discussions were held, in which Schönberg met
with his students, answered the questions that were
put to him, analysed compositions and talked over
matters of art. In these discussions a desire to make
music soon developed, and also the desire to give a
hearing to those modern works which it had not been
possible to hear at regular concerts. But music was not
introduced merely with the view of making modern
composers well known—and here was felt the new,
didactic purpose of Schönberg—but in order that the
public might be educated to appreciate modern music.
In order to succeed in this aim of rendering new and
more difficult works accessible, a twofold plan was
necessary. First the works to be presented had to
be studied exhaustively and then so perfectly performed that the hearers could gain a clear impression.
Then the performances were to be repeated after a
short time, and, in the case of a complicated piece of
music, given three or four times, until the hearers were
imbued with the spirit of it.

With this end in view, the Verein für musikalische
Privataufführungen (Society for Private Musical Performance) was founded. It consists of a number of
people who pledge themselves as members for one year.
Regular weekly performances are given from the middle
of September to the end of June. The programme of
the works to be performed is issued at the beginning
of the concert. In these performances there is no one-
sided consideration of any particular "school," but
strict attention is paid to the presentment, in the most
comprehensive way, of the most important works re-
cently composed, in so far as this is possible within the
scope of a chamber concert. This scope has its limitations. The first to receive consideration are compositions
for piano, piano and voice, and works in a chamber
setting. Thus, a great number of Debussy's chamber
works have been performed, songs, *L'île joyeuse* and
En blanc et noir, and sonatas for violin and violoncello;
Ravel's string quartet, his *Gaspard de la Nuit* and
Trois poèmes; clarinet trio and piano pieces by Reger;
Bagatelles by Bartók; and a solo violoncello sonata by
Kodály. With the addition of harmonium, piano, solo
wind and strings, the *Orchesterstücke* by Webern, the
Lieder eines fahrenden Gesellen (*Songs of a Traveller*) by
Mahler, and Schönberg's *Fünf Orchesterstücke* were
rehearsed for an invitation performance of the society
in Prague. Individual orchestral works by Mahler,
Reger, Strauss, Debussy, and Ravel were performed on
two pianos. From ten to twenty rehearsals were devoted
to each work. The leader of the ensemble was responsible for these, though at the final rehearsals,
Schönberg himself directed.

Schönberg learnt this insistence on thorough rehearsals from Mahler, and he feels it his duty to hold fast consistently to the heritage he has thus received.

It is well known to what a wonderful height of perfection Mahler brought the Vienna Opera during the ten years of his activity. All who lived during his time apply to their idea of a perfect performance a standard quite different from that to which one is accustomed in ordinary practice. Schönberg has always taken care, in the performances of his own works, to get as near perfection as possible, by preparing beforehand so thoroughly that nothing is left to chance. Lack of experience in conducting originally stood in the way of realising this aim; but the more opportunities he had of appearing at the conductor's desk, the more perfect became his performances. Thus he was the more able to express what was clear in his mind.

An example of this kind of preparation is to be found in those rehearsals which preceded the performance of the *Chamber-Symphony*, given in the spring of 1918. The aim in view was to give those who found the work interesting, and wished to understand it, an opportunity of studying its construction from beginning to end under his direction. But owing to the fact that no opportunity for a public performance arose, the work was completely excluded from the ordinary scheme of concerts. Similarly, in the spring of 1920, Schönberg arranged to admit a number of musicians to the rehearsals of the *Gurre-Lieder* at the Opera House, although this was contrary to the bureaucratic regulations of the institution.

From all these characteristics one can recognise in him a man who, thinking not of himself, places the cause he has at heart before all; one who does not desire to surround himself with a halo, but gives freely of his spiritual possessions. He knows that he does not work in vain, that "the impulse that comes from a teacher returns to him again," and that in this way something new and vital is always coming to life.

"This book I have learnt from my pupils,"—so begins the preface to the *Harmonielehre*, the book in which Schönberg has recorded his ideas and experience in harmony. It is a book for pupils; it promises no more than it can give, but gives much more than it promises. This book goes more deeply into the essential nature of music than any other textbook; in it there is nothing to be learned of the "eternal laws of music"; one learns to think and investigate.

It is easily understood that this book has met with much adverse criticism from theorists; that to the conservatives it was too audacious in its setting aside of authority, and that to others it offered too little advice on "modern" compositions.

However, as a teacher, Schönberg is opposed to premature theoretical formulation; he has an aversion from people who have a good knowledge of modern theory before they have composed, and also for those with whom what is new is not the expression of experience, but the result of speculation. It is remarkable how carefully he proceeds in the chapter of the *Harmonielehre* in which he speaks of new chord-formations. For how can we see clearly here, when we really have no satisfactory explanation of the harmony of Bach, of the later Beethoven, Schumann, Wagner, and Brahms?

That the theorists are not in agreement with the *Harmonielehre* should not be to their discredit, in the light of passages like the following:

No art has been so hindered in its development by teachers as music, since nobody watches more closely over his property than the man who knows that, strictly speaking, it does not belong to him. The more difficult it is to produce proof of possession, the greater is the attempt to furnish it. And the theorist, who generally is no artist, or a bad one (which comes to the same thing), has therefore every reason to take the trouble to make himself secure in his undeserved position. He knows that the pupil learns most through the examples that the masters give him in their masterpieces. This the ordinary teacher feels, and attempts to find some compensation by setting theory, an abstract system, in the place of a living example.

Schönberg sets himself in opposition to the power which the theorist seeks to turn into security for himself by means of a bond of union between himself and the æsthetician. How little imposing it sounds, if the teacher tells the pupil that one of the most advantageous means for the attainment of the effect of musical form is through tonality, and how very different it sounds if he speaks of the *principle of tonality* as of a *law*.

Therefore, to put it more clearly, he is against giving to the teaching of musical science the importance of fundamental ideas. According to Schönberg's view, music belongs to the explanatory sciences which teach us what a thing is and not how it ought to be done. Every preconceived theory tends to exercise compulsion on new phenomena and on works of art, and it is only phenomena that can be taken for granted.

How can we say, That sounds good or bad? Who is judge in this case? The authoritative theorist? He says, even if he does not justify his opinion, what he knows—that is to say, not what he has discovered for himself, but what he has learnt; or what everyone believes because it is everyone's experience. But beauty is not the experience of everyone, being at most only the experience of certain individuals. Above all, if such a judgment be allowed to stand without further justification, it must needs be of such an axiomatic nature as to be readily admissible.

This marks the beginning of Schönberg's positive work, an example of which I should like to add. It treats of a prohibition in the teaching of harmony which has caused young musicians a good deal of mental worry: the question of consecutive fifths.

It is forbidden to proceed from one fifth to another on the ground that such a progression sounds crude. Schönberg regards this explanation as quite false, and seeks for another. For how should consecutive fifths in themselves sound bad, since people certainly sang parallel fifths for centuries? But there is another consideration. They were superseded by other progressions and they fell into disuse, " so that the ear was prepared to find such combinations new and even surprising. The contrary, however, was the case; they were old, but forgotten."

Schönberg advised his pupils to adhere to the prohibition so long as they were learning; later they could override it. But it would be senseless to remove this prohibition altogether, while adhering to other regulations in harmony. One might say to pupils: Every combination of sounds, every progression is possible, but we are not yet far enough removed from things at the present moment to determine the conditions under which this new process should be carried out. Therefore, he advises his pupils to go the way that the development of harmony has taken.

If a student learns harmony mainly out of interest in works of art, he will derive only a better understanding of the masterpieces of art. It is, therefore, immaterial to him whether, in the short time he devotes to the production of music, the exercises he does are modern or not. Yet it may be of importance for him that the instruction he receives leads him to regard the bringing forward and encouragement of other artists as necessary factors in the element of beauty, even though the ears of old-fashioned musicians might be horrified thereat. But if he is a composer, he should wait quietly until he discovers in which way his development and nature are impelling him, and he should not desire to write music, the responsibility for which can only be borne by some mature personality: music that artists, almost against their will, have written in obedience to the impulse of development, and not as a result of an unchecked persistence in uncertainty of form and purpose.

I think these remarks throw an illuminating light on Schönberg's work. There is nothing in him (as there is nothing in any great and sincere art) *pour épater le bourgeois*: on the other hand, there is none of the joy in upheaval and revolutionary activity with which so many young artists seek to intoxicate themselves. He attempts to adhere to the traditional so long as it is best for him; only when his whole nature strives against it, when the impulse within is overpowering, does he decide to forsake the traditional path and strike out new ways for himself.

In this connection, mention might be made of a passage in an essay on *Musikkritik* (*Musical Criticism*), which Schönberg wrote in 1909 for the musical periodical *Der Merker*:

Characteristic of our time is the breaking away from " premises." The colossal production of " Weltanschauungen," philosophic views of life, of new, overwhelming philosophic and artistic movements, is the product of mistaken individualism, the individualism of Philistines, which is responsible for an over-estimation of originality, which prevents us from arriving at a clear and tranquil view of things, and from a slow and careful examination. In the *status nascendi* every new truth apparently opposes all that one believed formerly, and gives the impression that it can solve all the problems concerning which mankind has hitherto occupied itself in vain. And it almost looks as if such acquired culture were an actual impediment, as if the person most capable of applying and expounding a new teaching were he who knows nothing of its rudiments. To such a one these ideas that are struggling for recognition never appeal in vain. As a result the layman is a factor in cultural life, who can wound the creative artist with a cruelty almost equal to that of the professional.

Quite apart from the occasion of this quotation, this passage contains much that is characteristic of Schönberg. Like all significant natures he finds himself deeply rooted in the spirit of his time, but he strives to reach out in every direction by means of his own creative powers. A smaller personality, on the other hand, when he has succeeded in making only one step into unaccustomed regions, thinks that he is already completely free from all restraints and is inclined to overrate the importance of the achievement. Hence the frequent contradiction to be found between the theoretical postulates of the "programmists" and the real creators, which in times of artistic revolution is apt to disappear.

All the passages in the *Harmonielehre* that contain such reflections attempt to remove the contradictions between the old and the new. And with this end in view Schönberg did not amplify the passage where he speaks of modern harmony in the new edition that appeared in 1923, but expanded the chapter on modulation.

The discussion on dissonance is of very great importance. Schönberg points out the difference between it and consonance, and he defines consonance as the closer and simpler relation with the ground-note, and dissonance as the more remote and more complicated. Thus he holds by a graduated distinction between consonance and dissonance. The consonances turn out to be the first over-tones; the nearer they are to the ground-note the more productive they are. The more remote the over-tones, the less they can be made to fit in with a combination of sounds, and the more they need resolution.

Through the removal of the distinction between consonance and dissonance, the æsthetic evaluation, which has gradually been losing ground, of consonance as being beautiful, and dissonance as being ugly, disappears altogether. For if the distinction no longer exists, if dissonances are merely more remote relations to the ground-tone, where does beauty end and ugliness begin?

Beauty appears only from the moment when the unproductive begin to miss it. Before that point it does not exist, for the artist has found no conscious need of it. He is satisfied with truthfulness, with having expressed himself, and having said that which had to be said according to the laws of his nature. The laws of nature manifested in a man of genius are but the laws of the men of the future; the hostile attitude of the mediocre towards them is sufficiently explained by the fact that these laws are good. Opposition to the good is so strong an impulse in the unproductive that, in order to conceal their emptiness, they yearn after beauty, which genius bestows unconsciously. But beauty, even if it does exist, is intangible; for it is only present when one whose intuitive power is strong enough to produce it, creates something by virtue of this intuitive power, and he creates something new every time he exercises that power. Beauty is the result of intuition; when the one ceases to be, the other ceases also. The other form of beauty that one can have, which consists of fixed rules and fixed forms, is merely the yearning of one who is unproductive. For the artist this is of secondary importance, as indeed is every accomplishment, since the artist is content with aspiration, whereas the mediocre must have beauty. And yet the artist attains to beauty without willing it, for he is only striving after truthfulness.

Among the most beautiful sections in this book, which is full of extraordinary thoughts and ideas, are those in which Schönberg treats of certain chords in Bach and Mozart and finds in them the precursors of appoggia-tura chords, ninth-chords and fourth-chords. When one looks at the musical examples given, one is amazed at the inexhaustible source from which these many hundred solutions are taken.

Only occasionally does Schönberg give examples from his own works: e.g. an inversion of the ninth-chord with the ninth in the bass, which, theoretically, does not exist, but which appears in the sextet; so that Schönberg says he understands the excitement of that concert society which rejected this sextet because it contained this chord. Of course, there is no such thing as the inversion of a ninth-chord, and, in consequence, no performance, for one cannot perform anything that does not exist! And so he had to wait for many years.

But if one goes through the works of his first period up to the quartet, Op. 7, and others of this period, for example, the chorus *Friede auf Erde,* Op. 13, and the two *Ballades,* Op. 12, one can easily see how closely the examples in the *Harmonielehre* are connected with his work; how they are "discovered," and bear the stamp of personality. Later on in this book, when several of the works, and especially the last-named vocal compositions, are under discussion, more may be said on the subject.

What I have here said concerning the *Harmonielehre* has been of necessity quite superficial. For it is impossible to give a survey of this exhaustive work, which fills five hundred pages, without writing a whole book on it. But perhaps through the extracts I have given I have succeeded in letting the author himself speak, and in showing that the *Harmonielehre* goes far beyond the limits of an ordinary instruction book, containing as it does a conception of art so serious and profound that it cannot fail to impress every unprejudiced reader.

There is another field of Schönberg's work that should be mentioned, for it forms a bridge, so to speak, between his theoretical and purely creative activity. This is the arrangement of a number of symphonic works of the Viennese Pre-classical composers for publication in the *Denkmäler der Tonkunst in Österreich (Monuments of Music in Austria)*, which was edited by Guido Adler, the director of the department of Musical History in the University of Vienna. This work belongs to the time of the completion of the *Harmonielehre*. Guido Adler had approached Schönberg with the request to collaborate with him in this volume, which was to treat of Viennese instrumental music in the eighteenth century. Schönberg undertook one half of the arrangements, the organist, Josef Labor, the other. They were published in the nineteenth annual series, vol. 39, in 1912, and contained symphonies, concerti, and divertimenti of the important composer, Mathias Georg Monn, and of Johann Christoph Monn—probably a brother of the former. Monn's influence on the Viennese classical writers, Haydn and Mozart, is here quite obvious.

In this volume, Schönberg, has added the cembalo part to four of the published works of M. G. Monn, a symphony in A major, a concerto for clavicembalo in G minor and one in D major, and a violoncello concerto; also to a divertimento by Johann Christoph Monn.

Perhaps a few words of explanation are necessary. In the orchestral and chamber works of the seventeenth and eighteenth centuries, up to the time of Haydn and Mozart, only the leading parts were written out, the sustaining chords that the classical writers apportioned to the wood - wind being given to instruments that supply the harmony, in particular to the cembalo. The musician who played the cembalo part was generally the conductor. He had before him only the figured bass part, and he improvised the successions of chords according to the rules of general or figured bass. Upon his capacity and imagination depended the more or less successful performance of the filling-in part. On no account—thus it may be gathered from numerous indications given by the theorists—was it an empty series of chords, such as one often finds in the new editions of the old works. The cembalist had to supply far more than a mere filling-in of harmony in all such places, in particular where the orchestra, through the movement of the parts, becomes weaker.

Schönberg's conception of his work was to adopt the attitude of a cembalist of the highest quality, and the results of his labours are miniature works of art. His masterly command of the material is recognised at once in the fugal *Allegro moderato* of the A major symphony. He takes themes that have appeared in the orchestra, puts them into the middle parts contrapuntally, needless to say with a virtuoso treatment in the symphonic work

that was still foreign to Pre-classical times. On account
of the liberty he thus takes, Schönberg has been frequently attacked, but, oddly enough, not by the music-
historians. For through the working-out of the figured
bass adopted by many arrangers, whereby just the
bare harmonic structure was revealed, people had become accustomed to quite a different conception of the
music. But if one studies the arrangements of works of
that time made by Hugo Riemann, one comes across
similar liberties taken by this researcher, who had a
sense of style, although they do not show the touch of
genius that is seen in Schönberg's work.

The violoncello concerto is much more simply
arranged, so that the virtuoso passages for the 'cello
might not be covered up. Schönberg has also arranged
this concerto for 'cello with pianoforte accompaniment.
In this original form it was performed at a Festival Concert in honour of the 20th anniversary of the *Denkmäler
der Tonkunst in Österreich*, which was held on November 19th, 1913, and at which the 'cello part was played
by Pablo Casals, accompanied by a small orchestra under
the direction of Franz Schalk. The Viennese composer,
Hans Gál, played the cembalo part as arranged by Schönberg. This concerto, which has something of the feeling
of Handel, deserves to be played more frequently.

Especially free in style is the arrangement in the con-
certos for clavicembalo, where the instrument that plays
basso-continuo is almost in rivalry with the solo cembalo
itself. In the divertimento for two violins and violoncello, the cembalo part has something other than a merely
accompanying rôle, and is itself independent, having
melodic influence as in a piano-quartet of Haydn.

These works have been published, though they are

E

not easily accessible. They seem to me, however, to be of real importance for the understanding of Schönberg's activity as a teacher. For although within these limits there was little scope for independent achievement, nevertheless one perceives in almost every bar the hand of the mature artist.

HIS WORKS

It often happened that young people came to Schönberg and showed him, with certain pride, their first
volume of printed songs—no worse, perhaps better,
than most of those that are usually printed. On such
occasions Schönberg was always in a bad humour and
asked if they could not have waited until they had written
something mature, there being no necessity to publish
things that showed good intentions but insufficient
mastery of form.

This was the measure that he applied to his own works;
nothing was printed that was not absolutely mature.
And already the earlier songs bear the stamp of Schönberg's personality, even if the characteristics, that now
strike us as being of the essence of his individuality,
appear only occasionally.

EARLY SONGS

The two songs, Op. 1, *Dank* (*Thanks*) and *Abschied*
(*Farewell*), to poems by Karl von Levetzow, may be
distinguished at the first glance from all that was
produced in the same period, by the polyphonic
accompaniment in the piano, which is here treated quite
orchestrally. There are no empty passages for the left
hand, but only figures and motives and melodic counterparts, as for example in the first song to the words
" Schönheit schenkten wir uns im stets Wachsenden,

was ich mir vorbehielt, im Raumlosen," and in the second, "Ziehe weiter, heller Stern der Sterne."

In this second song the vocal part has already a characteristic melodic curve, which always tends away from the purely declamatory, especially in the passage "Der Alleinheit schwere Trümmer, Schmerzen wachsen" ("The bitter pains of loneliness increase"). In certain interludes, of course, the limits of piano-playing are greatly exceeded, so that we imagine we hear the arrangement of a song for orchestra; in this respect, as also in the treatment of the melody, they foreshadow the *Gurre-Lieder*, to which they form, in some measure, a preliminary study.

But as early as the songs, Op. 2, Schönberg had acquired for himself an individual pianoforte style. The development from the first songs to these may be regarded as characteristic of Schönberg's development; they are melodically and harmonically quite concise and precise. They represent the intermediate stages of the way he was to pursue; the contingent and unessential are omitted, and the expression is reduced to the tersest form.

From the first bars of the first of the songs, *Erwartung* (*Expectation*) by Richard Dehmel,

one is in the atmosphere. The succession of chords, the harmonic flow of which, melodically solved, is imitated by the voice, occurs again and again throughout the whole song, in accordance with the principle that every musical event must have its consequence, unless a deliberate contrast is to be indicated. Wonderfully foreshadowing all the daring devices of *Salome,* sound the glittering chords to the words "Drei Opale blinken" ("Three opals gleam"); they lead with growing intensity to a warm melody, which has been evolved out of the earlier harmonies and the flute-like arabesque.

The second song has quite a different setting from the first; the text is also by Dehmel, *Schenk' mir deinen goldenen Kamm (Give me thy golden comb).* It begins with a melody for the voice which has a wide curve, and goes from F sharp minor through some very bold modulations back to F sharp major.

Like the melody, which during part of its course
touches D flat major and passes through B and D
major in order to make a cadence in F sharp major,
the *cantilena* is also characteristic of Schönberg, and
is reminiscent of a type of *cantilena* that is to be found
in the *Chamber-Symphony*.

Then the same melody, after a short modulatory
episode, appears a tone higher; but it is varied in the
second half, and is brought back with passionate and
syncopated rhythm, after a long passage in the dominant, to F sharp major. The second half of the song
introduces a very tender motive,

which is made to alternate in different parts of the piano,
affecting, to a certain extent, the voice. It is merely a
curtailment of the upper melody in the first sequence of
chords, with which as a postlude the song comes to an end.

These few analytical remarks bring to light, though
in a superficial manner, something that is very striking
when one studies the songs more thoroughly. A detailed

analysis is out of the question in this place. However, these remarks may at least give an idea of the wonderful inner logic on which the songs are constructed; and they explain how it is that the oftener one plays and hears them the greater is the enjoyment.

The other two songs of this opus, *Erhebung* (*Exaltation*) by Richard Dehmel and *Waldsonne* (*The Forest Sun*) by Johannes Schlaf, in accordance with the poetic basis, are harmonically and melodically a good deal simpler than the first song. *Waldsonne* especially, with its magical pianoforte accompaniment, belongs to those compositions that gained for Schönberg his first devotees from among the wider public.

Among the songs, Op. 3, are three that, so far as style is concerned, belong to an earlier period and have a broad orchestra-like basis, which groups them rather with the *Gurre-Lieder*. They are *Wie George von Frundsberg von sich selber sang* (*How George von Frundsberg sang of himself*), one from *Des Knaben Wunderhorn* (*The Youth's Magic Horn*) by Hermann Lingg, and *Hochzeitslied* (*Wedding Song*) by Jens Peter Jacobsen. Nevertheless these songs are of overwhelming expression. The first, a powerful baritone song, leads to a very intense passage, "Zwar gross' Not, Gefahr ich bestanden han, was Freude soll ich haben dran!" ("I have been in sore trial and danger, what joy is mine!"),

... Ge - fahr ...   ich be - stan-den han, ...

and it sounds like a self-confession of the composer. The second is a strophic song with a fine melodic curve in strict form; and the third, like the first two, is a man's song full of obstinate passion.

Along with these songs, the three others of this collection betoken a progress in comparison with those of Op. 2. In these, one already begins to feel the wealth of contrast that is so astonishingly characteristic of Schönberg in his later works. Even the first, a humorous song, *Die Aufgeregten* (*The Excited Ones*), from the poem by Gottfried Keller, has many charming points of detail in the description:

> Eine Bachwelle und ein Sandhäufchen,
> Brachen gegenseitig sich das Herz!
> Eine Biene summte hohl und stiess
> Ihren Stachel in ein Rosendüftchen,

Und ein holder Schmetterling zerriss
Den azurnen Frack im Sturm der Mailüftchen.

A ripple in the brook and a little heap of sand lost their hearts
to one another.
A bee hummed drowsily and thrust her sting into the sweetness
of a rose.
A bright butterfly tore her azure coat in the violence of a May breeze.

In this the voices of Nature are heard with fascinating
subtlety, reminding one of the melodrama in the
Gurre-Lieder.

A song of mature beauty is the other song of Gottfried
Keller's, *Geübtes Herz* (*An Experienced Heart*). The
warm melody of the words "Einer Geige gleicht es, die
geübet lang ein Meister" ("Like a violin on which a
master has long practised"), is foreshadowed in the piano
part and continued up to the end of the song. But the
style of accompaniment is continually changing; it becomes heavier and then fades away, bringing fresh
counter-melodies, so that in spite of its simplicity a
continuous variety is produced.

The most powerful song of the whole series seems to
me to be *Warnung* (*The Warning*), by Richard Dehmel.
It is almost brutal in its power and passion, which completely accord with the text. The voice is more declamatory
than *cantabile*. The accompaniment is based on a single
motive of two bars, which is full of suppressed energy and
in the middle section allows of warm and tender variation.

Zwei blut-ro - te Nel-ken schick' ich dir   mein Blut__ du,

THE SEXTET, "VERKLÄRTE NACHT"

With the string sextet, Op. 4, *Verklärte Nacht* (*Transfigured Night*), Schönberg created his first great work. Through his many youthful works, sketches and the unpublished string quartet, he was now sufficiently experienced in the problems of form that arise in writing for strings. Inspired by Dehmel's poem he wrote, at a time when all the young composers of modern tendency were producing operas in the Wagnerian style or symphonic poems for a large orchestra, a work for chamber-music of the most individual character and entirely new, in the sense that he applied the idea of the problem of programme music to the intimate sphere of the string sextet.

People who hear this work nowadays will find many connections with Wagner, for at that time musicians were so much enthralled by the novelty of Wagner's personality that it was almost impossible for a composer to avoid certain progressions that are to be found in Wagner. At the time, however, when the work appeared, nobody noticed these connections, but they felt the harmony was too daring and they were confused by the part-writing, which to-day seems perfectly clear and logical. They held aloof from the problems of the programme idea, and were especially hostile to the attempt in this particular work; they heard nothing but entirely new sounds and combinations that were unlike anything in contemporary music. As might be expected, the setting of a programme to music, and especially in a youthful work full of the zest of life, has made the music of *Verklärte Nacht* something unusually dramatic; so much so that one could wish in many places for greater fulness and strength of tone. Hence, when this work is played in large halls, it is a good idea to increase the number of performers. This certainly reduces the intimate effect of certain passages, but, on the other hand, it gives to the whole a far greater intensity, bringing out more clearly the flight and *élan* of the composition.

The structure of *Verklärte Nacht*, in accordance with the poem, is made up of five sections, in which the first, third, and fifth are of more epic nature and so portray the deep feelings of the people wandering about in the cold moonlit night. The second contains the passionate plaint of the woman, the fourth the sustained answer of the man, which shows much depth and warmth of understanding.

Over a heavy and frequently recurring low D rises the first theme, which at the same time embodies the atmosphere of the whole work. It is a sustained melody suggestive of deep sorrow:

Without any increase of strength it rises to the highest positions in the violins and finally comes to an end with a poignant chord. A tender thought now appears, which, however, is not further developed; and on a short, gradually increasing *crescendo* the passionate plaint of the woman begins, full of remorse:

> Ich trag' ein Kind und nit von dir.
> Ich geh' in Sünde neben dir.
> Ich hab' mich schwer an mir vergangen.
>
> I carry a child which is not thine,
> Sin-laden I go with thee;
> I have done myself great wrong.

A restless, palpitating motive forces its way from the depths and leads, by means of a rugged *crescendo*, to an overwhelming climax and then subsides. Now there is heard a tender dialogue, expressive of pain, between the 'cello and the first violin; and from this episode there is formed a lengthy development, which rises to a lively movement and proceeds from the hitherto steady 4-4 time to triple time, and then forms, from the early theme for the first violin, a new and expressive idea:

The tempo varies considerably, becoming sometimes quicker, sometimes slower; the movement then returns to 4-4 time, and again rises to a sustained climax, passing into a new and exceptionally tender *cantilena*, which reflects the verse that speaks of the longing for maternal happiness:

This theme is of such wonderful clearness and warmth, and is conceived on such large lines, that one is more than amazed at the constructive power of the twenty-five-year-old composer of this work. The "expressive" idea now follows, introducing a transition that leads to a repetition of the *cantilena*. It remains predominant and is followed by a *crescendo*, which rises to a climax that comes abruptly to an end. Then follows a section surging with passion, in which mysterious strains are interrupted by a wildly careering violin figure. The movement whirls restlessly on and ebbs again until, after a wild flight, it breaks with increasing speed into an enormous *fortissimo*.

Now the third section begins, introduced by a recitative on the first violin, the motive of which, taken over later by the viola, leads to the recurrence of the original theme, this time fully harmonised and acquiring thereby an overwhelming force.

After a few tender violin passages and the softest of chords in the highest positions, with which this picture of moonlit night closes, the fourth section begins with the comforting reply of the man:

> Das Kind, das du empfangen hast,
> Sei deiner Seele keiner Last.

> May the child thou hast be no burden to thee.

With a pathetic motive in the 'cellos, supported by full, clear harmonies, this section begins and proceeds to a magical picture which is intended to suggest the atmosphere:

> O sieh, wir klar das Weltall schimmert!
> Es ist ein Glanz um alles her.

> See how brightly the world gleams;
> There is radiance all around.

It begins with harmonics and muted passages for the violin; then the second violin and the first viola carry on an undulating movement, accompanied by the second viola (*pizzicato*), while the second 'cellos give the harmony in long-drawn-out *pizzicato* chords. Above all this appears a wonderfully inspired melody, *innig, sehr zart und weich* (with deep feeling, tenderly and softly), for the first violin:

The score can give only a faint suggestion of the wonderful effect of this passage; one must hear it to feel its beauty. The dialogue between violin and 'cello, corresponding to the voices of the man and the woman, rises continuously. It is interrupted by a suggestion of the first tragic theme, now faintly heard, in the highest notes of the first violin, the other instruments playing quite softly at the finger-board. The dialogue begins again, accompanied by a new theme in the first violin, which leads later to an expressive melody.

It first appears in the violin:

A restless insistence on the part of the 'cello interrupts this development and introduces fresh passionate feeling, in the course of which the various motives combine with one another. Among all these parts there hovers,

dominating the whole, the recitative-like motive of the
man. With the tranquil grandeur of this motive all the
restlessness disappears, and there begins the final section of the work, which corresponds to the last section
of the poem:

> Er fasst sie um die starken Hüften,
> Ihr Atem küsst sich in den Lüften,
> Zwei Menschen gehn durch hohe, helle Nacht.
>
> He seizes her boldly;
> Their breath mingles in a caress,
> And the two go forth into the bright night.

The dialogue between the first violin and the 'cello
again suggests the atmosphere of moonlight, while the
second violin carries on a sparkling accompaniment.
An infinitely delicate picture is conjured up thereby,

which, becoming enhanced, leads on to the combination
of the two chief themes. Then there follows, accompanied by chromatic harmonies, the first tragic motive,

which, now relieved of its melancholy, sounds as if removed from the earthly plane. Gradually the heights become clear and the thicket shining in the moonlight becomes visible. Now Nature is speaking; with the purest, subtlest touch the music now paints the picture of the thicket standing alone in the clear light. In a shimmering melody the happiness that the two people have found is reflected; then it dies away, and in the highest harmonics this tone-picture comes to an end.

In the case of this sextet, and also of the big symphonic poem, *Pelleas und Melisande,* likewise in one movement, which will be referred to later, the poetic idea is embodied in a happily conceived form. However closely Schönberg has here followed the course of the poem, his unusually strongly developed architectonic sense prevented him from letting the form lapse into a fantasy. There is certainly an excess of climax in the sextet, but that is attributable rather to Schönberg's exuberant fancy, which had so much to say; yet he never loses himself in mere externals, and the description of Nature is never an end in itself. Everything is seen and shaped from a central point. The present generation has quite rightly turned against external description in programme-music. The phase was necessary in order to bring forth the full beauty of orchestral tone, but this aim having been achieved it lost its justification. In both cases, while Schönberg has made use of the poetic outline, he has so conceived the things from within, that the music is fully justified, even if one does not know the "programme." To him the art of expression is all-important, as indeed it is in the case of every great art. When anything has an "impressionistic" effect (I take this word in the depreciatory sense that it has acquired among the moderns), it is due to the fact that the public sees first the husk and only later the kernel.

Furthermore Schönberg, in the section of the *Harmonielehre* that deals with the fourth-chords, has in a fine piece of writing explained why new attempts in art, at their first appearance, tend towards "Impressionism."

Adolescent sounds of what is in process of becoming —all feeling without a trace of conscious thought. Still in close connection with the embryo, which is more intimately bound up with the Universe than is our consciousness, it is nevertheless as such already a sign of a differentiation that will later produce something individual—something that differentiates itself because it is differently organised. It is an indication of possibilities that later become certainties — a premonition concealed in dazzling mystery. And since these possibilities belong to that which unites us to the Universe, to Nature, they nearly always appear at first as the expression of the voice and mood of Nature.

THE GURRE-LIEDER

The *Gurre-Lieder*, Schönberg's most comprehensive work, have no opus number. They follow the sextet, and are the composition of a man of six-and-twenty years. As a result of the amazing facility that enabled him to write out most of his compositions in an incredibly short time, these songs are, for the most part, the creation of a single spring and summer, the finale of the third belonging to the March of the following year. For the performance, Schönberg had created an immense framework, the like of which had not existed before, and even later was not surpassed by Mahler in

F

his *Eighth Symphony*. The third part of the poem itself
suggested an enormous apparatus, the *Wilde Jagd* (*The
Wild Chase*) offering great opportunity for a massed
choir and orchestra.

Schönberg employs, besides five solo voices, three
four-part male choirs and a mixed choir of eight parts.
The orchestra consists of four piccolos and four flutes,
three oboes, two English horns, three clarinets, two bass-
clarinets in A or B flat, two E flat clarinets, three bassoons and two double-bassoons, ten horns, six trumpets,
one bass trumpet, one alto trombone, four tenor trombones, one bass trombone, one double-bass trombone,
one double-bass tuba, six timpani, one bass-drum,
cymbals, triangle, glockenspiel, side-drum, tenor-drum,
xylophone, gong, four harps, celesta, some large iron
chains, and a large body of strings.

The setting for the wood-wind makes it possible to
allot each chord to its own tonal group. But whereas in
the first part the orchestration throughout is warm and
full, indeed at times overpowering for the solo-voice, in
the third part, especially in the passages of the work that
were orchestrated later, the orchestration is fascinating
in its novelty and of a kind hitherto unknown. Even if
one calls to mind all the great masters of the modern
orchestra, there is nothing to be compared with a piece
like *Des Sommerwindes wilde Jagd* (*The Summer Wind's
Wild Chase*).

The *Gurre-Lieder* consist of three parts, of which the
second part forms merely a transition to the third. The
first comprises the story of the love of King Waldemar for
Klein-Tove, and concludes with the song of the Forest
Dove, which tells of her death. Between the second
part and the third, which describes the "wild chase,"

there is only Waldemar's song in which he rebels against
God. The portrayal of Nature occupies a large place in
this work. The beginning of Waldemar's first song:

> Nun dämpft die Dämm'rung jeden Ton
> Von Meer und Land,
> Die fliegenden Wolken lagerten sich
> Wohlig am Himmelsrand.

> The twilight hushes every sound on land and sea;
> The fleeting clouds have gathered on the horizon.

inspired Schönberg to write an orchestral prelude in
which the twilight is portrayed. It begins with an E
flat major chord with added sixth, which acquires thematic significance. It is melodically accompanied by the
flutes, and in the seventh bar the first trumpet enters
with a theme derived from the first chord.

This introduction as a piece of tonal painting is a
deeply inspired conception.

At first there is only a triplet movement for flutes
over a chord sustained by two oboes, to which eight
second violins play an accompaniment. To this are
added two piccolos and two flutes, which play in
syncopated quavers, and a chord on the harp and semi-
quaver figures in the first violins. Into this texture of
chords the first trumpet enters with the theme, repeat-
ing it and introducing a short episode, while three
harps support the harmony. The horns are now added
with light chords, the first violin with long-sustained
notes, and the trombones with sombre tones. The

atmosphere of the piece is now interrupted by delicate chromatic chords, and the music proceeds to D flat major. The thematic combinations become richer and more complex, and ultimately return, only in a lower position, to the movement of the beginning.

Thematically the first song is in intimate relation with the introduction. It is replete with the sweet and gentle melancholy of eventide, and is very lightly scored for wood-wind, horns and strings. After Waldemar's song comes Tove's:

> Oh, wenn des Mondes Strahlen milde gleiten,
> Und Friede sich und Ruh durch All verbreiten.

O! when moonbeams gently shine, and all around lies tranquil peace.

Over this song the magic of moonlight is again outpoured. Only a few of the wood-wind instruments support the music, and the strings, all muted, play as solo instruments. The first solo violin and the first solo 'cello proceed in imitation and surround the melody of the song with a wondrously beautiful and lightly-moving theme.

The song dies away in the gentlest tones; the episode leading to the next song of Waldemar is already filled with raging unrest, such as is expressed in the song *Ross! mein Ross! was schleichst du so träg?* (*Thou, my steed, why dost thou tarry?*).

The music portrays all the phases of his hurried ride, without ever forsaking the formal structure of the song. It reaches the culminating point in the call of Waldemar, accompanied by the orchestra in its most glorious brilliance: " Volmer hat Tove gesehen " (" Volmer has seen Tove ").

In the song which embodies Tove's answer, the impulse initiated in Waldemar's song is continued. The orchestra has the same themes as before, but in what wonderful contrast they are! For here everything is differently conceived; the scoring is of the very lightest, and only in the concluding episode does the orchestra reach its full power.

As if coming from another world, Waldemar's song is now heard:

> So tanzen die Engel vor Gottes Thron nicht,
> Wie die Welt nun tanzt vor mir.

Even the angels before God's throne dance not as the world now dances before mine eyes.

This is a graceful melody of almost folk-song character, wonderfully harmonised. The inner voices of this three-part song have each a theme of equal importance, and yet the whole sounds quite simple and plain.

Tove's love-song forms a complete contrast to this:

The melody, the deeply-moving character of which no words can describe, is in its construction thoroughly characteristic of Schönberg. Its cadence has parallels in the *Traumleben* (*Dream Life*), and in a movement of the *Chamber-Symphony*. The widely-extended intervals already foreshadow the *melos* of the later works. The manner in which the orchestral parts play round the song and, by means of slight melodic and rhythmic variations, throw fresh light on the voice part, is also characteristic of Schönberg's polyphonic mode of thought.

Tove's love-theme now becomes the chief theme of the whole work. In countless variations, sometimes as the leading theme and sometimes appearing as a subsidiary theme, it reappears and generates through its pregnant melody the psychological association.

In Waldemar's song, "Es ist Mitternachtszeit und unsel'ge Geschlechter stehn auf aus vergess'nen, eingesunk'nen Gräbern" ("It is midnight, and unhallowed creatures rise out of forgotten and neglected graves"), a more sombre tone becomes intermingled with the bright colours that have hitherto prevailed. Ghostly sounds in muted violins and trumpets paint the picture of approaching misfortune, and sorrowfully Waldemar sees that his destiny is being fulfilled.

After this dark premonition of death, Tove's song proceeds to an ecstatic longing for the end; "Denn wir gehn zu Grab', wie ein Lächeln, ersterbend im seligen Kuss" ("We go to the grave as with a smile, expiring in a holy kiss").

It is scarcely possible in a few words to point out the wealth of construction in this song; the passage for the strings at the words "Die leuchtenden Sterne am Himmel droben" ("The stars shining in the heavens above"), the canonic imitation of the first violin and 'cello in the hymn-like song, *So lass uns die goldene Schale leeren* (*Let us drain the golden bowl*), which is accompanied by two harps, first and second violins and violas divided fourfold; and the sublime song at the end, which by rhythmical alteration gradually passes from common to triple time.

The last of the group of love-songs is Waldemar's, a song filled with sublime peace:

> Du wunderliche Tove!
> So reich durch dich nun bin ich,
> Dass nicht einmal ein Wunsch mir eigen.

Thou wonderful Tove!
Through thee have I become so enriched,
That not even my wishes are my own.

The music is relieved of all burden of earthly existence

when it portrays the peace that has found its way to the soul of Waldemar through Tove. The orchestra, in a long interlude, continues in this atmosphere and then proceeds, as the development of the first part, to luxuriant combinations of the chief themes. The music increases in intensity and later becomes almost dramatic in character when it assumes a tone charged with deadly fate, giving warning of Tove's approaching end. This message is brought by the Forest Dove, whose song, conceived on a large scale, is interrupted by short introductions to each verse which paint with wonderful orchestral skill the cooing of the doves. On account of the freedom of detail with which the song is treated, it has a definite, outspoken "ballade" character; thus, for instance, where it describes the funeral procession:

and tells of the queen who, with revenge in her heart, stands aloft on the balcony. The episode that follows sounds like a folk-song:

but from the basses there comes the sound of bells, overwhelming in force, in which the plaintive cry of the forest dove is heard, "Helwigs Falke war's, der grausam Gurres Taube zerriss" ("It was Helwig's falcon that cruelly lacerated Gurre's dove"). With this warning of death the first part closes.

The song of the Forest Dove, together with the preceding orchestral movement, forms so close a unity that the two have frequently been performed together apart from the rest. In this case also it is impossible, without going into detail, to give more than a superficial explanation. But even those who know nothing about the rest of the work, who do not perceive the art that pervades the whole, will nevertheless be touched by the grandeur and noble pathos of the music, and will feel its significance.

The second part, which is made up entirely of the long-drawn-out plaint of Waldemar, begins with a short orchestral prelude, developed out of the heavy chords with which the first part concluded, and also with a sorrowful theme for oboes, clarinets, bassoons, and horns, developed out of the song of the Forest Dove. It rises, employing several motives of the ballade, to a climax of powerful chords which introduce Waldemar's song:

> Herrgott, weisst du, was du tatest,
> Als Klein-Tove mir verstarb?

> O God! knowest Thou what Thou didst
> When Thou didst take Tove from me?

The accents become more and more poignant until Waldemar passes to the proud, "Herrgott, ich bin auch ein Herrscher" (" O God, I also am an over-lord "), which is supported by solemn harmonies for trumpets, horns and trombones, and ends in a passionate outburst.

With the sombre theme that had led first to Waldemar's midnight song:

Sehr langsam

the third part of *Die wilde Jagd* begins. As if from forgotten and neglected graves, there comes the sound of the muted chords of the Wagnerian tubas, which from here onwards are used more frequently.

Immediately the full orchestra enters and Waldemar's voice breaks forth with " Erwacht, König Waldemars Mannen wert" (" Awake, thou worthy of King Waldemar's men "), and then culminates in an outburst at the words "Heut ist die Ausfahrt der Toten" (" To-day the dead arise "), which is followed by a wild passage for the orchestra.

The scene with the peasant who watches the wild chase is here introduced as an episode. Here also much careful attention is paid to detail, and there are in particular many novel effects in the orchestra. Thereupon the choirs begin with their wild chase. Since the scene with the vassals in *Götterdämmerung* no music of similar, almost barbaric force has been created. However complex and involved the canonic imitations in the voice parts, the choruses, supported by the brass at their full power, sound perfectly simple and make an immediate appeal.

By this time the spectacle has come to an end, and Waldemar is heard to sing while the strings play the yearning Tove theme:

> Mit Toves Stimme flüstert der Wald,
> Mit Toves Lächeln leuchten die Sterne.

> The forest whispers with Tove's voice,
> The stars gleam with her smile.

This arresting song is followed by the grotesque song of Klaus the Fool, which is announced by a bizarre figure:

From here onwards one notices the difference in orchestration, especially in comparison with the first part. The orchestration itself forms a support for the polyphony. The middle voices in all their fulness are themselves set in motion; and from the instruments the utmost in compass, character, and capacity is extracted.

With a peculiar effect of the strings played "col legno," the Fool begins his song:

col legno am Steg.

He seeks to absolve himself from the curse of damnation, pointing out his honourable conduct in life:

He reviles his lord and king and yet reckons on being accorded a place in heaven. The passage that now follows for the orchestra belongs to the most *virtuoso* music ever written for an orchestra. It is an indescribably brilliant piece of unheard-of timbre, full of ideas and inspiration.

Waldemar subdues him; then another Fool also rises up against his lord and master and threatens:

> Du strenger Richter droben,
> Du lachst meiner Schmerzen,
> Doch dereinst, beim Auferstehn des Gebeins,
> Nimm es dir wohl zu Herzen:
> Ich und Tove, wir sind eins.

> Thou strict judge on high,
> Dost Thou laugh at my pains?
> Yet when once our bodies rise again,
> Mark well—Tove and I shall be one.

But morn begins to dawn, and the nocturnal spectacle loses its power. The choir sings softly.

The grave calls again to the restless sleepers who long for peace, and the scene gradually dies away in the mysterious depths of the double-bassoons and the double-bass tubas.

With soft but light tones throughout, *Des Sommerwindes wilde Jagd* begins with four piccolos, three flutes, oboes, clarinets and bassoons.

   ·   ·   ·   ·   ·   ·

I feel that this melodrama is the key to the understanding of Schönberg's later works. As he already expressed it in the passage in the *Harmonielehre* mentioned above, whatever is new arises first from a cosmic feeling, from the relation of the ego to the world. Here Nature is seen through the soul's experience. Waldemar's feelings are also those of the listener, towards whom there emerges from the sounds of Nature the voice of Tove.

It was a touch of genius to enhance the effect of the final chorus by conceiving the last piece before the chorus as a melodrama. And later on, this is the form of expression that constantly attracts and inspires Schönberg, for *Pierrot Lunaire* and passages in the *Glückliche*

Hand are melodramatic in character. Here the element of the orchestra is treated as a body of solo instruments so that the speaker may not be " covered." It is quite impossible to go into particular examples; I might, however, refer to the passage,

> Still! Was mag der Wind nur wollen?
> Wenn das welke Laub er wandet,
> Sucht er, was zu früh geendet.

Still! What is the wind's desire? When he turns the withered leaf, he is seeking something that has faded all too soon.

in which solo violin, solo viola and clarinet repeat continuously Tove's love theme; or

> Auf luft'gem Steige wirbelt er frei.

> On spacious path he whirls around.

where Schönberg, in a passage of ten bars, conjures up, by means of a figure for the flutes, a picture that is comparable with the magic tones of Debussy, and without dwelling for long, he proceeds with abundant exuberance to something new. For, beginning with the episode that immediately follows:

a rise to a climax is prepared, which ultimately leads to the final chorus, *Seht die Sonne*. On the word "Sonne" the final theme enters brilliantly on the trumpets, this theme harmonically corresponding to the beginning of the first part. Whereas in that case it appeared as the E flat chord with an added C, here it appears as the C major chord with the added A. In both cases I prefer, on account of the melodic significance, to regard the chord not as a six-five chord, but as an E flat major and a C major chord, prepared and resolved at the same time; since the choral movement ends with the simple resolution of A to G, and the C major tonality is also preserved in the scale at the close.

Following the purely harmonic entry of the choir is a movement unusually rich contrapuntally, *Farbenfroh am Himmelssaum* (*Rejoicing in celestial colour*). An episode appears in the shape of a light and lively melody which is imitated in all the voices. This movement and the episode interchange.

The finale of the whole work is thus formed by means of broad harmonies on the theme-chord C–E–G–A, which rise to a climax. This theme and that in the finale are intertwined and then reappear in every bar. In the brightest and most glorious magnificence, as a hymn to the ever-returning sun and to the awakening of all the dead to new life, the *Gurre-Lieder* are brought to an end.

PELLEAS UND MELISANDE

Once only did Schönberg, following the example of his contemporaries, write a symphonic poem; but even in this instance he has so treated the problem that the carrying out of the idea was compatible with formal construction. *Pelleas und Melisande* was written after the drama by Maurice Maeterlinck, on which Claude Debussy at about the same time wrote an opera. The musical course of Schönberg's tone-poem follows more or less the chief scenes in the drama.

The introduction describes how the ageing Golo finds the lonely Melisande in the forest. With the first notes the tragic character of the work is fixed, and Schönberg at once raises his work above the level of the ordinary tone-poem. He is not content to remain on the surface in the treatment of his work, by merely describing episodes in the course of the drama. He goes to the very depths; he considers not only the fate of the individual characters, but also the nature of fate itself. He is not concerned merely with the incident of Golo's meeting with Melisande in the forest, but also with the fact that their coming together is charged with fate. A "programmist" composer, misunderstanding the application of the principles of the Wagnerian music-

drama to symphonic music, would have attempted to
give a description of the forest in which Golo had
strayed. With Schönberg, however, the description is
inward. A sombre theme (a), which is frequently interrupted by another fateful theme (b),

begins low down in the bass, and gradually rises. It
represents, as it were, a difficult conflict, as if the music
were to make known the torment of soul in which Golo
is involved. Then begins, *a little quicker*, a tender theme,
first in the oboe and later in the English horn.

It is Melisande's first vision; nevertheless a sombre
atmosphere is predominant until Melisande's theme,
in *stretto*, is heard. But it would be an error to regard this
theme as a tonal description in the sense of a *leitmotiv*.
The psychological significance of the passage is parallel
to that in the treatment of the *Tove* motive in the *Gurre-
Lieder*, in the section entitled *Des Sommerwindes wilde
Jagd*:

>   Still! Was mag der Wind nun wollen?

G

In that example it is the consciousness of the omni-
presence of the Supreme Being; but in the case of Melisande it is the picture hovering before the mind, and
now becoming realised in a dream with its various
shapes, that has become true; and then again Schönberg gives expression to the exuberant power of the
musical visions which in their opulence force themselves upon him.

How rich his fantasy is in combination may be seen
from the page of the score here reproduced, which
will give an idea of the passage in question better than
any verbal description.

Along with the Melisande theme, which is heard
alternately in the three oboes, cor anglais, E flat clarinet
and bass clarinet, appear accompanying chords in the
bassoons, and the bass is supplied by a sequential figure
developed out of the first sombre theme. In addition to
this texture of parts there comes a broad expansive
theme, softly played by three horns, which is to char-
acterise Golo.

Here already we have an example of Schönberg's
procedure by abbreviation, whereby after the sounding
of the themes in succession he allows them to appear
simultaneously. As in the works of the later period a
chord is often nothing other than the *verticalisation* of
the idea which was first conceived *horizontally*, so in
this instance he strives by means of polyphony to substitute for a successive form of musical procedure one
that is simultaneous.

With the climax of the Golo theme at the two *forte*
bars played by the full orchestra, the end of the introduction is reached and the chief theme of the symphony begins expressively and broadly (*sehr warm und*

PELLEAS UND MELISANDE

in breiter Bewegung). In regard to the orchestration of
the introduction, the following should be noticed. The
darker and more delicate orchestral colours are alone in
evidence. The first and second violins are omitted
throughout the whole introduction; from the wood-
wind, the flute, and from the brass, the trumpets and
trombones, are absent. The horns, up to the entry of
Golo's theme, are heard in their lowest register. Con-
spicuous are muted violas and violoncellos, clarinets in
the middle register, and the oboes in singularly bright
contrast.

Now there begins in the violins a broad melody,
symbolical of the way in which Golo leads the princess
to the royal castle and takes her to wife.

The secondary theme of the symphony is introduced
by a transition which suggests that something fateful
has entered into the life of both. Pelleas is characterised
by a bold, soaring theme, which, beginning *heroically,*

undergoes a *passionate* continuation in the wood-wind, horns and strings.

The first part is immediately repeated by horns in imitation, and out of the second part, material is taken for a rise to a climax in the basses, which is twice interrupted by the melodic contrast of the Melisande theme. The orchestration of this passage is highly individual. The Pelleas theme appears in the trumpet, supported by chords in the *pizzicato* strings, while figures in the clarinet and *staccato* passages for the horns accompany it. It is an exposed passage and needs great care to interpret rightly. At its repetition it is easier to perform, since the theme now lies in the horns and the accompanying figure has become both richer and more flowing.

Following on the lyrical part comes a reprise in which, after the development of the Golo theme, a new Melisande theme appears. This section leads to the second part of the work, the Scene at the Well. Formally it corresponds to the scherzo of a symphony, although the scherzo character is only maintained at the beginning of this part. For as a background to this scene is conceived the ride of Golo, who falls from his horse at the moment when the ring falls into the well.

A short interlude expressive of Golo's awakening suspicion of Melisande and Pelleas leads to the Scene at the Castle Tower, which here, as also in Debussy's opera, marks a climax. Over tranquil chords in the horns and bassoons, varying forms of the Melisande and Pelleas themes are delicately combined. The Pelleas theme appears in flutes and clarinets in its shortest form, while two solo violins play it in its full form. As a middle voice there appears in the clarinets the theme that portrays Melisande's awakening love, to which is added, in the solo 'cello, the Pelleas theme. From this combination are developed tones of extraordinary tenderness and beauty, to which the following scene, corresponding to the reprise of the scherzo, is in violent contrast.

The Scene in the Vaults may be regarded as the second trio; instrumentally it is among the most daring music hitherto written for the orchestra. Here are heard the strange *glissandi* in the trombones, which are so produced that the ground-tone is fixed with the lips while the slide is put through all positions in such a manner that the chromatic, as well as the intermediate semitone and quarter-tone intervals, are clearly heard!

With this, so far as its content is concerned, the second part ends; formally, however, I prefer to regard the introduction to the Scene at the Well which now follows, and which in character belongs to the scherzo part, as the real finale. Thus this piece falls into five parts.

Following on this, and representing the adagio of the symphony, comes the Farewell Scene between Pelleas and Melisande, a wonderfully tender and long-drawn-out *cantilena*. This part is the most extensive of the whole symphonic poem. It introduces the different themes and combinations, though all within the scheme of the adagio. Towards the end it rises to a climax of ecstatic expression.

But Golo waylays the lovers and kills Pelleas; with this begins the fourth part of the symphony, which like-

wise forms a grand reprise of the whole work. Here
also appear two new themes which are introduced
episodically. Parts of the introduction to the first movement and also of the adagio reappear; then there
follows the scene in the death-chamber of Melisande,
in which the Melisande theme, augmented by trumpets
and trombones, sounds like a chorale over a pedal-
point in harps and basses. Here Schönberg made use
of the whole-tone scale at a time when it was not yet
known in Germany.

The epilogue, beginning with the broad *cantilena* of
the first theme of the chief movement, introduces, in
new combinations, the most important themes of the
work. They are for the most part in their shortest form.
Moreover this final movement, regarded from the point
of view of form, has the character of a final exposition.
Gradually the polyphony dies away, the tension is relieved and, becoming softer and softer, the work closes
with the first figure of the chief theme, with which the
theme of fate is intertwined, thus linking together
beginning and end.

For this tone-poem, written in one movement and lasting an hour, Schönberg makes use of a correspondingly large orchestra: four flutes, three oboes, cor anglais, E flat clarinet, three clarinets in A and B flat, one bass-clarinet, three bassoons, double-bassoon, eight horns, four trumpets, one alto-trombone, four tenor trombones, one double-bass tuba, two pairs of timpani, percussion, one glockenspiel, two harps, and a large body of strings.

Pelleas und Melisande is one of the most polyphonic works ever written for an orchestra. It is astonishing how each theme is enveloped in counterpoints, and how the theme itself is involved in imitation; furthermore, how in the development of the parts huge melodic complexes are combined one with another. Thus, for instance, in the Scene at the Castle Tower there are no fewer than five themes which themselves undergo manifold imitation one with another.

On looking back, one sees that after this work a continuation in the same direction was, for Schönberg, impossible. He had reached a summit beyond which he could not go! A new way had to be opened up, a way that Schönberg found in his middle period through the employment of strict form. At this time he stemmed the stream of his exuberant fancy, and arrived at the suppression of all that was merely episodical, such as is to be found in his earlier works. Thus he attained to the technical mastery which gave him, in the works of his latest period, the necessary assurance, untrammelled by any form, to create something from within.

SONGS

Before Schönberg turned his attention to these new problems, there appeared the *Sechs Orchesterlieder* (Six Songs with Orchestra), Op. 8, and the *Acht Lieder für Klavier und Singstimme* (Eight Songs for Piano and Voice), Op. 6.

As early as the *Orchesterlieder* one cannot but notice an essential simplification and concentration of style. The scoring consists of one piccolo, two flutes, three oboes, three clarinets, three bassoons, four horns, three trumpets, three trombones, three timpani, bass-drum, triangle, cymbals and a large body of strings. But this material is seldom used altogether. Before all else it serves to facilitate a variety of combination.

The words of the songs are by various authors and musically they have very varied settings. The simplest of all is the third, *Sehnsucht* (*Longing*), from *Des Knaben Wunderhorn*, which approximates to a folk-song, the orchestration of which, moreover, is very delicate in style. It is a sustained song, somewhat after the manner of a *Ländler* (country dance), but, like all songs of this epoch, written with an extreme regard for the harmonic relations within the scale.

The second of the series, *Das Wappenschild* (*The Coat of Arms*), a stray number from *Des Knaben Wunderhorn*, is, in contradistinction from the first-named, a stormy song almost inclining to the dramatic intensity of the ballade, strongly orchestrated and having a wide sweep.

The rest of the songs are very different from those just mentioned: the first, *Natur*, by Heinrich Hart, with its cosmic tranquillity and solemn harmonies for the wood-wind, horn, trumpets and harp; and the fourth to the sixth, which are settings of poems by Petrarch.

These songs breath warmth and maturity. The string part is polyphonically maintained, but the polyphony is not felt as such, nor does it turn out to be more than is necessary for the enlivening of the voices. Of these songs again, the fourth and fifth, *Voll jener Süsse (Full of that sweetness)* and *Nie ward ich, Herrin, müd' (Never was I, O lady, tired)*, stand in close connection. In them, possibly for the last time, full and flowing sounds of the orchestra are employed with the sonorous tones of horns and trumpets, as in the first part of the *Gurrelieder*. Already the last one, *Wenn Vöglein klagen (When little birds make their plaint)*, suggests the first traces of the characteristic orchestration of the later works, as does the handling of the orchestra as a body of solo instruments, which forms a bridge to the instrumental treatment in the third part of the *Gurre-Lieder*; so also the law of declamation is no longer of paramount importance, but gives way to the melodic idea necessitating a musical rather than poetic disposition of the chief voice.

With the introduction and establishment of this principle, the supremacy of the orchestra over the vocal part—a feature of post-Wagnerian music—comes to an end. For the orchestra is no longer merely the vehicle of feeling, but it gives support to the vocal part, which henceforth becomes musically the chief part.

The way for this new principle of style was prepared in the *Eight Songs*, Op. 6, although it does not appear so clearly in all as in the first song, *Traumleben (Dream Life)*, by Julius Hart, in which the progression of the intervals, supported by the harmony, is of extraordinary intensity.

Es ruht auf meinem Mun - de ein Frühling jung und warm

Here also is to be found the most complete regard for harmonic relations, which are kept strictly within the limits of the tonal cadence.

The remaining songs represent rather a continuation of the way that had been opened up by the songs of Op. 3. They are all built on a piano accompaniment founded on a theme which, by means of a pregnant formula, seeks to embody musically the essence and the content of the poems. Such, for instance, are the delicate, mysterious *Alles* (*All*) by Richard Dehmel, *Verlassen* (*Forsaken*) by Hermann Conradi, with its wonderful rising sweep at the words "Entgegen dem jungen Maientag" ("Towards the dawn of May"), where the music glows and sparkles. Such, furthermore, are the intimate *Ghasel* by Gottfried Keller, the passionate *Am Wegrand* (*By the Wayside*) by John Henry Mackay, the mysterious *Lockung* (*Enticement*) by Kurt Aram, and the culminating point, *Der Wanderer* by Friedrich Nietzsche.

The songs are among the most compact and the most unified that were produced on the lines of development from Schumann through Wolf. Written with the means at a composer's disposal in the first decade of the twentieth century, they surpass everything that has been created on these lines, through their logically developed musical ideas and through the personality that is behind every note. At first they aroused incalculable hostility; but thanks to the indefatigable support of a small circle of singers, among whom were Frau Winternitz-Dorda, Frau Gutheil-Schoder and Frau Emmy Heim, who performed his songs long before they became accepted, they gradually became more popular and are now widely approved.

In the earlier years of the twentieth century, the culminating point of the movement, which under the
influence of Wagner's music and teaching in regard to
music drama had led to free forms of fantasy, had
already passed in Germany and Austria. Moreover, in
the symphoni˙ poems the free form of music had been
discarded, and an attempt had been made to become
more architectonic and to base music on the traditional
classical forms. Influenced by the example of César
Franck and his school, in which all the movements of a
symphony are united through a single principal theme,
variously treated—and this form of technique goes back
through Liszt to Berlioz—Richard Strauss gives to his
Heldenleben (*A Hero's Life*) the form of a symphony
with a principal theme running through it, and he is
even more true to this form in the *Sinfonia Domestica*,
in that all the movements are connected with one another and the relations between all the parts are of the
closest. Schönberg has employed the same principle of
form in his chamber-music.

First String Quartet, D Minor

The *String Quartet*, Op. 7, like the sextet, *Pelleas
und Melisande*, and the *Chamber - Symphony*, is performed without a break. This quartet consists of four
movements: allegro, scherzo, adagio and rondo-finale.
Of greatest significance, however, is the first part, in
which the chief themes of the work are treated to
a broad exposition, which foreshadows all the other
movements. Between the separate movements, parts of
the first are interpolated; furthermore the thematic

38307

material of the second, third, and fourth movements is to some extent already existent in the first, so that it is permissible to speak of a single movement from which had been formed a scherzo, adagio, and rondo.

Reduced to a scheme, the following represents the plan of construction:

I

1. (*a*) Group of chief themes. (*b*) Transition. (*c*) Group of secondary themes. 2. The first development.

II

1. Scherzo. 2. Development. 3. Repetition of the group of principal themes.

III

1. Adagio. 2. Repetition of group of secondary themes. 3. Transition.

IV

1. Rondo-finale. 2. Development of earlier themes. 3. Final section.

As in the broad plan, so in detail the art of varying the themes and the interrelated parts is carried out. The whole work, lasting forty-five minutes, does not contain a single inner-voice nor a single figure that is not thematically conceived. For example, the principal theme,

Lincoln Christian College

of the first movement appears with a bass which apparently has no other function than to provide the lower notes. But as early as the first reappearance of the theme in the thirtieth bar, where it is given to the 'cellos and transposed to E flat minor, this bass part is given to the violins according to the rules of double counterpoint; curtailed and changed into 3-4 rhythm, it plays an important part in the further course of the work.

The secondary theme, the entry of which is effected out of one of the transition groups, appears accompanied by a second part.

One gradually recognises it as the principal theme, whereas the part played by the first violins forms the second part to the theme, the secondary section. This secondary section now undergoes the most varied transformations until, appearing in an energetic 3-4 rhythm, it forms the chief theme of the scherzo. A similar relationship exists between the principal theme of the adagio and the rondo-finale.

Yet with all this it must not be supposed that there is anything artificial or forced about this work. The quartet holds the continuous attention of the listener; melodically, harmonically and rhythmically it is so rich in variation that one is entirely absorbed when listening to it, and one allows no thought of the construction to arise. What would theory have to say in regard to the arresting beauty of this adagio theme?

The D minor quartet, thanks to the untiring efforts of the Rosé Quartet, which plays this work on all its tours, is one of the best - known compositions of Schönberg. Moreover, the Flonzaley Quartet, with performances in America, the London Quartet, with performances in England, and the Quatuor Lejeune, with performances in Paris, have all contributed much to making this work more widely known, and in recent times practically every well-known Quartet on the Continent has included this work in its repertoire.

How remote seems the time when this work was the subject of heated controversy, and when, as in Berlin, it was jeered at and declared to be a "pitiful negation of all art"!

Does this not give food for thought to those who to-day are so ready to pronounce judgment on the later works?

The Chamber-Symphony

Schönberg's next work, the *Chamber-Symphony* in E major, Op. 9, has a similar construction to that of the quartet, but is more concise in proportion, although the same wealth of thematic material prevails. The employment of more instruments, and also of instruments more strongly differentiated in tone-colour, gave the opportunity to carry out many transformations and combinations of themes simultaneously, whereas in the quartet this was only possible in succession.

The *Chamber-Symphony* is written for fifteen solo instruments, and is scored as follows: flute (interchanging with piccolo), oboe, English horn, clarinet in D and E flat, clarinet in A and B flat, bass-clarinet, bassoon, double-bassoon, two horns and string-quintet.

In this work, still more even than in the sextet, it has been found necessary, for performances in large halls, to increase the number of the strings, in order to balance to some extent the fuller tone of the wind. There is something else in favour of this arrangement. In compositions such as this, the unusual intervals demanded of the strings frequently affect the intonation, and this makes the understanding of the work extraordinarily difficult. When many are playing, discrepancies in intonation cancel one another; therefore, in first performances especially, the listener is greatly assisted in understanding the *Chamber-Symphony* when it is played by a large number of strings. On such occasions naturally a conductor is desirable; indeed, as the first performance in Vienna showed, he is indispensable even if the work is to be given in its simplest form, in which strings are represented by solo-players. Of course such

a performance demands wind-instrument players who
are thoroughly accustomed to chamber-music and solo-
playing.

The *Chamber-Symphony* is one of the last compositions in which Schönberg makes use of tonality. The
way in which he has enlarged harmonic possibilities
and formed new cadences betrays sovereign mastery.
Moreover, he has at the same time entered on the
path to a new region. Already in the opening bars a
chord consisting of five superimposed fourths appears,
which harmonically heralds the first theme of the
principal section, a passionate theme of aspiration for
the horn.

This theme, made up of fourths, plays an important
part in the course of the symphony: it appears at all
the important points of departure in the development,
and thanks to its peculiar composition it is capable of
discarding tonality and also, through its fanfare-like
character, of bringing into the polyphonic texture of the
voices a contrast that has immediate effect.

Directly after the horn theme, a short motive appears
leading to a cadence in E major; then follows the chief
theme, which is constructed out of a lavish use of the
whole-tone scale.

H

It is not alone the employment of a whole-tone scale that constitutes the novelty of the theme, but, above all, the concise and pregnant nature of its conception. For one must remember that at this period the "*grosse Melodie*" (see the first theme of the *Heldenleben*), was predominant.

Here Schönberg had already found a way to a concise form of theme-construction, the like of which he had not quite fully achieved in the string quartet. This, by the way, is an example of the "untheoretical" nature of each of Schönberg's ideas. Still involved to some extent in the practice of his time, Schönberg strove to work out this thematic idea and to develop it in the accepted way, until after some days he saw that the theme *must be* exactly as it had occurred to him, and that his inspiration was different from that of his contemporaries.

The recognition of this was of decisive importance for Schönberg; from that time onward, he followed the dictates of the voice within and severed all connection with the traditions of the past. This represented the real liberation of his nature from ties that were only an impediment to his development.

His labours at the *Chamber-Symphony* gave Schönberg a decisive impulse in search of a new style of orchestration. All that he has orchestrated since the *Chamber-Symphony* bears the stamp of being written for solo-players; that is to say, every instrument in the orchestra attains to importance and is treated in accordance with its nature. The problems to be faced in a composition for ten wind instruments and five strings had the effect of maturing this new principle in orchestration, and quite early in these works they led to a most highly individual colouring.

FRIEDE AUF ERDEN

In this period, falls the composition of the chorus *Friede auf Erden*, Op. 13, and of the two *Ballades*, Op. 12. These works represent the highest point in Schönberg's endeavour to discover within the scope of tonality the most distant harmonic relations, but they are essentially more conservative—if I may use this word—than the *Chamber - Symphony*. The chorus is pre-eminently a masterpiece of polyphonic writing, containing a wealth of warm melody and infinite variety.

Four verses by Conrad Ferdinand Meyer afford the basis for the musical construction. The introduction of the second and third verses is indicated by a *ritardando* at the end of the one verse and a change of tempo at the beginning of the next verse. The fourth verse corresponds to the first, but is laid out on broader lines; themes from the second and third verses are used, and there is a broadly-conceived final section, which forms the crowning point of the whole. Noteworthy is the frequent employment of the voice-parts in thirds, which produces the effect of chords.

The refrain of the first, second and fourth verses —"Friede, Friede, auf der Erde" ("Peace, peace on earth")—gives opportunities for similar formations in the music; but they are in each case varied, and the tonal relations, especially in the cadences, are expanded to an extraordinary degree. An example of this is afforded by the conclusion of the first verse with the extended D major cadence.

A similar example is to be found at the close of *Jane Grey*, the first of the two *Ballades*, Op. 12. Here likewise there is a long-drawn-out D major cadence, the ultimate resolution of which is postponed until the very end. These two *Ballades*, the opus number of which is confusing, since it gives the impression that they were written after the *Drei Klavierstücke*, are related, so far as style is concerned, to the *Sechs Orchesterlieder* and the *Acht Lieder*, Op. 6, which are followed almost directly by the first *Ballade*.

In keeping with the character of the *Ballade* as such, they are even simpler in melody and accompaniment than most of the last-mentioned songs. Hence one feels, when one takes into account the development of Schönberg's creative activity as a whole, the tendency to loosen the harmonic texture and to exceed the ordinary limits of tonality.

The harmonic construction of the following example will present no difficulties to the readers who know Schönberg's *Harmonielehre*; indeed, it affords an opportunity of seeing more clearly in practice what he has laid down in theory, and shows, as has been mentioned already, how closely the relations between theory and practice have been maintained in this work.

THE SECOND QUARTET, F SHARP MINOR

There is one more work on a large scale that forms the bridge between the works of the earlier and later styles: the *Second Quartet* in F sharp minor, Op. 10. Here the new tendencies become more obvious, and in the final movement one can clearly recognise the complete change in style.

In contradistinction to all other instrumental compositions hitherto considered, this F sharp minor quartet consists of four movements, of which the first three are kept in strictly classical form, the fourth being more freely conceived. Moreover, the third and fourth movements have in addition a vocal part written to poems by Stefan George.

The very first theme with which this movement begins, without any preparation, is wonderfully unified and concise.

The B sharp is enharmonically changed to C, which at first becomes the fifth of a passing F minor chord and then the third of an A minor chord, with which the principal theme appears a second time. Immediately after the return to the principal theme the secondary section appears, which in its turn is followed by the first theme. This theme, as before, leads by means of a parallel transition to a varied repetition of the secondary section, in which a short two-bar figure enters; out of this figure the final group is developed. Both

development and recapitulation are likewise carried out
with much conciseness.

The scherzo is a strange, elusive piece in which there
are traces of scurrilous humour, which later is in particular evidence in *Pierrot Lunaire*; thus, for instance,
when towards the end of the trio the song *Oh, du lieber
Augustin, alles ist hin* (*O my dear Augustin, all is over*) is
heard in distorted form. In regard to technical construction it represents the perfecting of the technique
derived from the classics.

From the artistic point of view, the most perfect
movement of the quartet is the slow third movement;
in this there is a wonderful combination of the *lieder*
form with the *adagio* form with variations. The theme
of the variation is a period of eight bars consisting of
two sections.

The first section consists of two motives, of which
the first (I.) is taken from the principal theme of the
first movement, the second figure (III.) being taken from
the scherzo; both then undergo transformation. The
parts accompanying the first figure (II.) consist of varia-

tions of the secondary theme of the first movement. The second section (IV.) is an augmentation of the final group of the first movement.

After the statement of the theme, there begins a repetition of the first section, in which the parts are inverted; in the second section the voice introduces a new melody. The variations that follow, which are all in periods of eight bars, introduce variations of the different figures, while the changing moods of the poem are reflected in the thematic material.

In the last movement the lyrical nature of the poem and the consequent free treatment of the form appear in the foreground; and yet even here an exhaustive analysis would bring to light all manner of interrelations.

A long instrumental introduction precedes the beginning of the song *Ich fühle Luft von anderen Planeten* (*I feel air from other spheres*), in which entirely new tonal colouring is heard. In this instance all connection with tonality is completely given up, and the melodic curve has a freedom to be found nowhere else.

. . . .

With this quartet, which shows Schönberg in full possession of technical power, he abandons traditional form and devotes himself to new problems. And this it is which makes the decisive step. For in the first phase, Schönberg takes the accepted forms of his period ready to hand and contents himself with expanding them. In the second phase, which embraces for the most part instrumental works, he endeavours to attain to the highest completion of the classical form, by giving every part some thematic life and by fusing the transitions from one thought to another in the closest possible way.

In the third and last phase of development, Schönberg attacked simultaneously both problems, *i.e.* of
melody and form, attempting to combine them in an
entirely new manner. The melodic curve is now made up
of a number of small figures, so that it may be able to
follow the subtlest stimulus of feeling. These figures, like
the colour-spots in a picture,[1] seem at the first glance to
be indiscriminately juxtaposed; but when one views the
work in its entirety, they are seen to form an organic
whole, and produce a single unending melody which
at the same time is in keeping with the form of the piece.

The novelty of this kind of art consists in the fact
that the content is in keeping with the form of the piece,
and that neither themes nor figures are formed to be
developed later, but that every thematic element is a
self-contained entity and yet capable of being merged
with others into a higher unity with the whole.

One can well understand that a manner of speech so
individual and personal, which scarcely shows a single
connection with the works of other contemporaries,
offers far greater difficulties for general comprehension
than the earlier works.

Whatever may be our attitude to these works, one
thing is certain. An artist, who through the *Gurre-Lieder*
and the D minor quartet, which are now universally
recognised, has given proof of being in the front rank
of composers of the present day, can claim that we
should concur in anything that he now writes, or may
write in the future; and that we may be convinced that
it has its inner logical justification. It does not frequently
happen that a composer is so much in advance of his

---

[1] The author here refers presumably to the "blobs" used by the
painters who follow the methods of *pointillisme* or "divisionism."

time as Schönberg, yet it is not entirely unknown. In
the musical history of the sixteenth century, a remarkable parallel may be found in the case of the Italian
prince, Gesualdo da Venosa. At a time when chro-
maticisms made but a timid appearance in madrigals,
he developed chromatic progression to an extent not
to be found again until the later works of Wagner; but
his work remained entirely unnoticed.

Nowadays such isolation on the part of a creative
composer is no longer possible. Yet it will be some time
before what Schönberg has created will be felt by his
contemporaries as part of their own idiom and language.
But attention must be paid to the essential. What most
people regard as the chief factor in Schönberg's work,
namely the lack of concords and of a definite key, is
really only of secondary importance. The dissonant
harmony arises from the progression of the parts; it
could not be otherwise, because it is intimately bound
up with the melody. But it is well known that one
quickly accustoms oneself to new and unusual dis-
cords. The real difficulty of the new works lies more
in the comprehension of the progression of the individual
parts, and of their lapidary conciseness. For in his
new works, Schönberg can say in one single figure
what formerly required several bars to express; and
simultaneous sounds, a chord for example, may
often be a substitute for a succession of notes in a
melodic phrase.

The best way to an understanding of the new style
is to follow the chief parts in their development, regarding the secondary parts really as counterpoints whose
aim and object are to support the principal part: that
is, to concentrate on the chief event of the music and

not to suffer distraction. Thus one will realise how in atonal music, cadential progressions arise which one feels to be just as compelling as the cadences in tonal music; and also how the melody displays a tendency to rise to a point and then fall; in short, how also in this atonal music a system of law obtains, the rules of which for us, who are in the midst of the event, cannot yet be formulated.

I ought at least to attempt to approach from another side the principles of the new style. In the instrumental music of the nineteenth century, one may trace everywhere a tendency to construct the form of the music out of the means afforded by the symphony. Beethoven, as one of the pioneers, knew how to rise with the help of small figures to a powerful climax which grew out of one germ-motive, the stimulus of the idea. The principle of contrast, which is dominant in all art, first comes into its own when the effect of the idea of the germ-motive has ceased. The period before Beethoven knew nothing of such construction in the symphony. The themes of Mozart, for example, often contained within themselves the principle of contrast; they are compact first sections followed by freer second sections. This principle of a direct effect of contrast, and of a juxtaposition of contrasting figures in the course of the theme, is revived by Schönberg in the works of his later style.

He holds to a principle that the earlier composers abandoned, because they devoted all their intensity of creative work to the amplification of form. When this form had reached its fullest maturity, the time was propitious for reintroducing the earlier, more complicated form of melody-building which, although it did not make use of sequential progression towards a climax, nevertheless produced a form of its own.

All these theoretical considerations, however, have no meaning unless they arise out of some living work of art. They force themselves upon one solely as the result of a long occupation with the works themselves. They can give no idea of the essence of the work of art itself, for such can come from intuition alone.

PIANO PIECES

The pianoforte pieces, Op. 11, are the first work in the new style. They are atonal and do away with the idea of dissonance. This, of course, is the case with the works of the modern French and Russian composers. But these composers make harmony and the timbre of the pianoforte their point of departure, whereas in Schönberg's case it is counterpoint. Hence they arrive at quite different results.

I insert here the beginning of the second of the *Drei Klavierstücke*, in order to give those who do not know them some idea at least of what is meant when one talks of modern music.

But even to give this one example seems to me almost useless, in view of the wealth of thematic figures and designs that this music especially displays. It is best to take the *Klavierstücke* themselves and attempt to read them and follow the lines of the melody as well as their development, and then afterwards to play them through. It might even be better to begin with the *Sechs kleine Klavierstücke*, Op. 19, which are remarkably short, and which might be compared with the sketches a painter makes for larger pictures. In this way a certain rhythm is set up which itself becomes a motive—a figure that quickly passes and is self-contained. Thus with a few strokes a picture of commanding power of expression is outlined.

THE BOOK OF THE HANGING GARDENS

After the *Klavierstücke* come the *George Lieder*, fifteen songs from *Das Buch der hängenden Gärten*, Op. 15, which are preceded by the two songs, Op. 14, *Ich darf nicht dankend* by George, and *In diesen Wintertagen* (*In these winter days*) by Henckell. These two songs likewise represent a bridge between the old and the new song style, and are on that account, quite apart from their musical beauty, of great importance. In the songs from the *Buch der hängenden Gärten*, Schönberg has succeeded for the first time, as he has explained in detail in his analytical programme, in approximating to the ideal of both expression and form that had hovered before his mind for years. In actual fact the external scheme of these songs, which architectonically form a group, is entirely new. The pianoforte is no longer an instrument accompanying the songs, such as we find in the songs of Wolf, Strauss, and also in Schönberg's songs,

Op. 2, 3, 6, and 8, but is entirely independent of the vocal part. The piano part, however, does not keep up a single kind of movement or a theme with a consistent rhythm, but is perpetually new, introducing new figures and themes that are self-contained and call for no further treatment. It is no longer confined to providing *Klang* (tone-colour or timbre), but it undergoes a treatment somewhat like that in the *Bagatelles* of Beethoven; it introduces music for which a new kind of pianistic interpretation must be evolved.

A study of Schönberg's, called *Das Verhältnis zum Text* (*The Relationship to the Text*), which appeared in 1912 in the *Blaue Reiter* edited by Marc and Kandinsky (the leaders of expressionist painting in Germany), in which also the *Herzgewächse*, Op. 20, and songs by Berg and Webern were published, gives a detailed account of the way in which to combine words and music when writing a song. He describes in this essay how he had discovered, in certain of the Schubert songs, that he did not know what the poem was really about. When Schönberg had made a closer acquaintance with the poems, he found that he was still no nearer the understanding of the songs, nor had he arrived at an altered conception of the music.

Still more decisive than this experience was the following: Inspired by the opening sounds of the initial words of the text in the case of many songs, without troubling in the least about the course of the poetic events, indeed without being in the least concerned with them in the turmoil of composing, Schönberg had gone on writing to the end and had only discovered some days later what the poetic content really was.

Then to my greatest astonishment I discovered that I was never more faithful to the poet than when, led as it were by the first direct contact with the opening sounds, I felt instinctively all that must necessarily follow from these initial sounds. Then it became clear to me that it is with a work of art as with every perfect organism. It is so homogeneous in its constitution that it discloses in every detail its truest and inmost being. Thus I came to a full understanding of the Schubert songs, together with the poetry, from the music alone; and of Stefan George's poems from their sound alone; and this with a perfection that could hardly be attained by analysis and synthesis, and which in any case could not be surpassed. When one has once perceived this, it is easy to understand that the external agreement between music and text, such as is shown in declamation, tempo, and tonal intensity, has little to do with the inner meaning; that it is equivalent to the elementary imitation of nature embodied in the copying of a picture; and that an apparent superficial divergence may be necessary on account of a parallel procedure on a higher plane.

I quote these remarks, not in order to discuss their accuracy, which would be quite beside the point, since every artist must answer this question according to the laws of his own nature, but because they throw much light on Schönberg's creative activity; and for this reason are of the utmost value for us.

An example of the latest song style may be found in the opening bars of the fourteenth poem in the *Buch der hängenden Gärten*, which, with the delicacy of a breath, express the poet's awe in the contemplation of the mystery of Nature.

Another song, containing the words "Von Sternen feine Flocken schneien, sachte Stimmen ihre Leiden künden" ("Light snowflakes fall from the stars and soft voices make known their sorrows"), has a similar far-off atmosphere; and again in another song, *Als Neuling trat ich ein in dein Gehege* (*As a novice I come into thy enclosure*), there is a strain of mysticism. Then comes the song *Jedem Werke bin ich fürder tot* (*Henceforth I am dead to all work*), with its listless mood, and also the passionate *Wenn ich heut nicht deinen Leib berühre* (*If I to-day do not come nigh thee*). Thus everything has its particular stamp, its peculiar magic, into which one must sink oneself if one would grasp the whole. Only thus can the bewitching beauty of this music disclose itself to the appreciative listener. He feels the wealth, the soulful expression, the descriptive power, and the consummate art that penetrates both music and poetry of these songs.

THE FIVE ORCHESTRAL PIECES, OP. 16

In the *Fünf Orchesterstücke*, Op. 16, the new style is transferred to the orchestra. They represent something entirely novel, for the new style has radically changed the orchestration. The orchestra is treated purely as a

I

body of solo instruments; the chords are formed from
the most varied tone-colours, which are treated according to their natural intensity; and within the chords
themselves, certain tones are allowed to be more prominent than others. How this may be understood is
shown by the beginning of the second piece, in which
each note of the changing harmonies is played by a
different instrument.

Harmonically regarded the first piece is the simplest;
it is constructed on a logical and consistent bass motive,
which is sometimes augmented, sometimes diminished.
Here, by the way, is to be found the orchestral effect
that occurs later in *Die Frau ohne Schatten* (*The
Woman without a Shadow*), of Richard Strauss. In
the middle section there is a rise to a climax in which,
by means of flutter-tongueing (*Flutterzunge*), muted
trombones and the bass-tuba produce a tremolo with
their full power.

The second piece, as is shown by the example given
above, is of a lyrical nature. The middle section particularly is unusually soft and tender; it begins on a
theme for the solo viola which is taken up later by the
'cello. Then begins the episode in which the celesta
plays an imitative figure, accompanied by two flutes
alone. Into this texture there is brought a theme, light
and staccato, for the bassoon, which later on becomes

predominant and forms a counterpoint to the first lyrical theme of the middle section.

The third piece is purely harmonic and shows the same chord in a continually changing light. Schönberg gives the following indication as to the performance of the piece:

It is not the conductor's task in this piece to bring into prominence certain parts that seem to him of thematic importance, nor to tone down any apparent inequalities in the combinations of sound. Wherever one part is to be more prominent than the others it is so orchestrated and the tone is not to be reduced. On the other hand, it is his business to see that each instrument is played with exactly the intensity prescribed for it—that is, in its own proportion, and not in subordination to the sound as a whole.

This change of chords, which runs through the entire piece without any development of theme—a change so little noticeable that one is aware only of a difference of tone-colour—produces an effect comparable with the quivering reflection of the sun on a sheet of water. The piece owes its origin to such an impression at dawn on the Traunsee. The peculiar orchestration should be noticed: first of all two flutes and clarinets, then the second bassoon with the solo viola for bass. There follows the somewhat brighter chord for cor anglais, muted trumpets, first bassoon, horn and solo double-bass.

The fourth piece is of more passionate character; lively passages for the wood-wind and impetuous figures for the trumpets and trombones appear. The last piece on the contrary is, like the second, in lyrical vein and extraordinarily polyphonic. In this piece, Schönberg has introduced, for the first time, a sign to indicate which parts are to be regarded as principal parts; this he did in order to aid the conductor in reading the score. Schönberg has pursued this practice in all his later works, even extending its application, for this new orchestration makes demands on the conductor hitherto unknown. In a later work, *Vier Orchesterlieder*, Op. 22, he has even gone to the extent of taking special measures to reduce the external difficulties attaching to the reading and studying of modern scores. In this connection he has written a preface to the *Orchesterlieder*. After speaking of previous attempts to simplify the full score, and pointing out their unsatisfactory nature, he writes:

My experiment solves the difficulties in another and much more satisfactory way. For some time past I have written my first notation of an orchestral work on two, six, or eight lines, indicating generally at the same time the full orchestration. After a certain amount of reshaping and the introduction of slight alterations, this first notation, in conjunction with the ordinary manner of scoring (which I have always prepared in the old way, though with another end in view, *i.e.* merely to indicate the parts), serves as a basis for the setting up of the simplified *Studier und Dirigierpartitur* (Score for students and conductors), which I shall henceforth have published.

The principles are as follows:

1. The conductor's score should remind one of a piano edition arranged for two, four, or even six or eight hands, and with this end in view the manner of notation peculiar to such editions should be employed.

2. One should be able to follow the progression of each part at any time.

3. Where special complications make it necessary, the various groups, wood-wind, brass, percussion and strings, etc., should be kept separate, in order to facilitate the separate rehearsal of such groups.

4. Every point should be indicated in the simplest way possible. That is to say:

(a) Parts that are played by several instruments should be indicated once only.

(b) Parts that go in similar rhythm should, where possible, be tailed (abgestrichen) in common.

(c) Where possible the harmonies should be brought together as is done in piano-editions, so that one may have, as far as is possible, the whole chord together.

(d) Only so many clefs and staves should be used as are absolutely necessary for the representation.

These are the chief points that manifest the radical redisposition of the full score. Characteristic of Schön-berg's way of thinking is his attempt to remodel everything that implies unnecessary difficulty. How great in this respect is the difference between him and so many reformers in the matter of notation, whose "improvements" demand first of all the learning of a new "system," and whose consistent application would lead to the result that one would be unable to read any score written in any other way! After mature reflection I can heartily commend this unusually simplified notation for difficult works. For in this way the conductor can get to know them quickly and without difficulty, and after a certain amount of acquaintance with the works, it will not be difficult for him to conduct from the students' scores (Studier-partitur).[1]

[1] For further information on Schönberg's Simplified Score (Verein-fachte Partitur), see Dictionary of Modern Music (Dent & Sons, 1924), page 458.

ERWARTUNG

Subsequent to the *Fünf Orchesterstücke*, Op. 16, are the two dramatic works, *Erwartung*, Op. 17, and *Die glückliche Hand*, Op. 18. I have already mentioned in the first part of this book that the words of the monodrama *Erwartung* embody the problem of how to represent dramatically what may happen to a man in a moment of the highest tension and intensity of feeling. Marie Pappenheim, to whom Schönberg communicated this idea, has attempted to solve the problem by employing a number of scenes.

For this work, which is an original attempt to make one person bear the burden of the whole dramatic development, Schönberg has written for a large orchestra consisting of the following: one piccolo, two flutes, three oboes, one English horn, one D clarinet, one B flat clarinet, two A clarinets, one bass-clarinet in B flat, three bassoons, one double-bassoon, three horns in F, three trumpets in B flat, four trombones, one bass-tuba, one harp, one celesta, kettle-drum, glockenspiel, xylophone, percussion, and string-orchestra.

The scene begins on the borders of a forest. Roads and hills are lit by the moon; the trees of the forest stand lofty and dark. A woman clad in white comes in search of something; she is anxious and hesitating. " Hier hinein? Man sieht den Weg nicht " (" In here? One can see no way through "). With the softest tones the music attempts to portray this delicate, tremulous mood, which becomes more and more sombre. At last she takes courage and proceeds into the forest. While the scene changes the solo-violin, begins and carries on a dialogue with the bass-tuba and the clarinets, whose melody is prominent here. The second scene shows the forest through which the woman is feeling her way. Suddenly in her sorrow she remembers. "It was so quiet behind the walls of the gardens—no more the scythes were to be heard—no one called or moved—and the town in the bright mist—with longing I looked onward."

One is carried away by the beauty of this passage. A soft chord, played by oboe, muted trumpets and flutes, is heard accompanied by the violins with a tender melody, and is then followed by a melody for the flutes. At the word *sehnsüchtig*, two solo-violas and two solo-'celli sustain the theme while an expressive *cantilena* for the oboe hovers above, and is followed by wild passages for the clarinet. The effect of the whole is one of entirely novel tone-colour. The same may be said of every single bar of this wonderful score.

The scene again changes. The woman comes out of the darkness into the light of a clearing in the trees. Her anguish becomes more oppressive; she thinks she sees some creature and calls in despair for her lover. Again there is a change of scene, while the orchestra plays a motive gradually increasing from a *pianissimo* to the loudest *fortissimo*, then dying away.

The woman comes out of the forest on to the broad road on which moonbeams play, and behind which, in the background, a house is to be seen. She is exhausted; her clothes are torn, and her hair is dishevelled. Her face and hands are cut and bleeding. The undefined fear within her develops into anxiety for the life of her lover.

"I can go no further . . . no one will admit me . . . the strange woman drives me away! If he should be ill! A seat . . . I must rest . . . but I have not seen him for so long." Then she stumbles against some object and recognises her loved one dead at her feet. The orchestra has increased to its highest power and is then spent.

She will not believe that the dead man is her lover. And now, under the impression of this fearful event, she becomes the prey to wild imaginings. She talks to the dead man tenderly, coaxingly, moaning in her misery.

And then amid the searchings in her memory she realises more and more that between her and him, something estranging had arisen, something of which she had been ignorant but which she now begins to realise.

"Now I remember . . . the sigh in thy sleep . . . like a name . . . thou didst kiss the question away from my lips. . . . But why did you promise to come to me to-day? . . . I will not have it. . . . No, I will not. . . . Why did they kill thee? . . . Here before the house. . . . Did someone discover thee? . . ." And in her desperation she turns against the woman who has taken her lover from her. Then she is seized with melancholy.

"How deeply I have loved thee . . . I lived remote from all things . . . I have known none but thee . . . this whole year . . . ever since thou didst first take my hand."

Here throughout the softest and the most delicate tone-colour is used, the scene proceeding broadly and with much depth of feeling. A lightly whispered *parlando* follows when she, without a trace of hatred, thinks of the other woman. Her whole being becomes transfigured when she calls out: "My dearest, the morning draws nigh. . . . What can I do here alone? . . . In this endless life. . . . Light will come for all . . . but must I alone remain in the darkness of night?"

And now her thoughts fade into the distance. Morning comes and reminds her of the many times when they had separated and had bidden one another farewell. She thinks she sees her lover coming towards her. This pale visionary mood is portrayed with uncanny power in the music. Then comes the cry, "O bist du da—Ich suchte" ("Oh! Art thou there? I was seeking thee"). And with a ghostly chromatic contrary movement in the whole orchestra, which fades away into thin air, the curtain falls.

It is quite certain that nothing approaching this for daring and novelty has ever been written for the stage. For its production an entirely new conception of dramatic style is indispensable. The same may be said of the *Glückliche Hand*. But what stands out, above all the daring and novelty, is the overwhelming warmth and passion of this work, which was composed in a few days, almost in a condition of trance, and which was years in advance of its time.

Several attempts were made to bring about a production of *Erwartung*, but the undertaking had to be abandoned until 1924, because of the enormous difficulties that such a production entailed. However, at the musical festival in Prague in May 1924, Alexander v. Zemlinsky, the leader of the German opera, undertook the performance and prepared the work for rehearsal. For the part of the Woman he found a fine interpreter in Marie Gutheil-Schoder, who created a performance which ranks with her Elektra and her Potiphar. The production, which was surely mistaken scenically, showed how vivid and clear the music of this piece is, and how much it stands on a traditional foundation.

Nowhere else can we find music so vivid, original and full of emotion. The orchestration has a wonderful charm, and is woven round the voice with a new sound-effect of the subtlest refinement. The expression and effect of the work are quite extraordinary and one recognises that an addition of great importance has here been made to modern music, an addition which one can no longer afford to overlook.

THE LUCKY HAND

A similar attempt to arrive at a new form of dramatic art is embodied in the *Glückliche Hand*. In this work, for which Schönberg wrote both words and music, it is a man who sustains the whole of the action; but he is involved in ever-varying circumstances and events. The action is reduced to the most compact form, so that often one bar is sufficient to represent an incident, and already in the next bar something new is afoot.

Schönberg takes great trouble over lighting effects. Every scene has its special colouring, and within each scene itself the nuances of light change according to the mood.

The characters in the *Glückliche Hand* are two men and a woman. Six women and six men form a chorus. The woman and one of the men have only mimed rôles; for the other man's part, a high baritone is necessary. The orchestra is the same as that in *Erwartung*.

The first picture, in which the music begins with a lively movement for the bassoons and bass-clarinets, without introduction, shows the stage in almost complete darkness. A man lies in the front; on his back

there sits a fabulous cat-like animal, which seems to
have bitten into his neck. The background of the reduced stage is formed of dark violet velvet, in which
little holes have been cut. Through these holes the
illuminated greenish faces of the six women and the
six men appear. Half speaking and half singing, they
carry on the function of a chorus, which in this case
is the same as that in ancient Greek tragedy. Drums and
harps accompany with a triple movement, which is kept
up throughout the whole scene. The words express
sympathy for the fate of the man who longs for earthly
happiness, although it is supernatural happiness that is
vouchsafed him. There is a combination, in quite a
special way, of the weird *Sprechgesang* (song-speech),
with the actual singing.

The chorus comes to a close; the faces disappear;
the fabulous creature has gone; it is quite dark. Suddenly, from behind the scenes, loud, commonplace music
and the harsh laughter of a crowd are heard. Thereupon
the man rises with a bound, and stands upright in his
tattered clothes; at the same time the background has
opened out and the stage is full of light. This change,
made with the utmost dramatic fertility, is accomplished
in three bars.

Like a sigh, there now sounds the melody of the 'celli,

followed by a sombre and heavy chord for the four bassoons. Now for the first time the voice of the man is heard; a new and widely-extended chord of two clarinets and deep bass-tuba accompanies the voice, whereupon the orchestration undergoes a complete change. A bright melody for the flute is heard rhythmically accompanied by the celesta. It is continued in the next bar by the celesta itself; flutes give the chord, the melody being followed in this bar by the sound of the strings.

A young and beautiful woman appears and gazes sympathetically towards the man, who shudders without turning round. She offers him a goblet lighted by violet rays. The man slowly empties the goblet, but while he drinks, her face takes on a cold expression and she retires to the other side of the stage. The man stands deep in thought and sings:

Wie schön du bist. Ich bin so glück-lich, weil du bei

How lovely thou art. I am so happy, for thou art

mir bist! Ich le - be wieder. O du Schö - ne!

with me! I live again, O beautiful one!

There now appears close to the right side of the stage an elegant man, a "lord." (The musical illustration of this passage is individual in the extreme; there are high *tremoanldo* notes for sixfold divided violins, while in the viola there is a purely rhythmical motive.) He takes the woman, who hastens towards him, in his arms and flees with her. The first man sees this and groans deeply. The woman returns and appears to beg for pardon; but as soon as the man begins to regain confidence in her, the same thing is repeated and she once more eludes him. The man, however, does not notice that she has left him; he raises himself to his full height and sings " Nun besitze ich dich für immer " (" Now I possess you for ever ").

The scene rapidly changes. The stage represents a wild, rocky landscape, which is built up as a plateau. From out of the ravine there towers up a piece of rock, the size of a man. Behind are two grottos. The man emerges from the ravine with a bloody sword in his hand; an incisive, rhythmical motive on the low notes of the wood-wind, harp and strings portrays his approach. The grottos are flooded with light, and one perceives in them workmen who are labouring with files and hammers. The man approaches, takes a piece of gold and lets the hammer fall heavily. The anvil breaks in two beneath the weight of the blow, and from the fissure that is made, the man takes a richly bejewelled diadem. The workmen threaten to rush at him, whereupon he hurls the precious object at them with a laugh. The grotto becomes dark again.

Now begins the most extraordinary part of the drama. A wind rises and gradually increases in violence; at the same time there is a *crescendo* in the lighting effect. It begins with a touch of red light, passes through brown into a mottled green, and from thence into a dark blue-grey followed by purple. This is followed by an intensive dark red which becomes brighter and more glaring. From this it passes, through orange and bright yellow, to blinding light.

This *crescendo* in light and wind is meant to give the impression that it comes from the man. From lassitude his condition passes gradually into one of growing excitement, and when the yellow light appears it would seem as though his head would burst.

The music of this scene is based on a motive of three notes, which appear harmonically in two different positions.

Here the music represents a purely harmonic, instrumental idea similar to that in the third of the *Orchesterstücke*, Op. 16. The volume of sound gradually increases until, at the climax, it is played by the trumpets in imitation at their full power. Then the storm of colour and tone gradually subsides. The light changes to a mild blue, while delicate sounds are played on the wood-wind and celesta, and the solo-violin plays a graceful melody in three-eight time.

The woman appears with the other man; the first man attempts to reach both of them; he creeps up, but all in vain. He tries to woo the woman, but she has nothing but contempt for him. Thereupon he once more clambers after her. He climbs up to her; but she pushes the rock, which suddenly begins to glow from within, and assumes the shape of the fabulous animal in the first scene. The rock falls on him, so that he is buried under it. At this moment, darkness supervenes, and the commonplace music and harsh laughter are heard again behind the scenes. As soon as light appears, the scene is found to be the same as the first. The man lies under the fabulous animal, and the six men and six women sing a recitative, passing on to a *cantilena* of growing intensity.

"Musstest du's wieder erleben, was du so oft erlebt? Musstest du? Kannst du nicht verzichten? Nicht dich endlich bescheiden? Ist kein Friede in dir? . . . Fühlst du nur, was du berührst?" ("Hast thou again to experience what thou hast so often suffered? Canst thou not be resigned? . . . Is there no peace within thee . . . Dost thou feel only what is near?")

The singing ends in a whisper: "Und suchst dennoch! Und quälst dich! Und bist ruhelos! Du Armer!" ("Seeking ever to grasp what must always elude thee! Tormenting thyself! Ever without rest, poor one?")

I am fully aware that it is scarcely possible to give, through this account, more than a mere suggestion. In the case of a dramatic work that demands such an unusual scene and enhances the effect of the music by

means of colour, one can gain a complete impression
only by seeing it on the stage.

The first production took place on October 14th,
1924, in the Musical and Theatrical Festival Room of
the Volksoper in Vienna. Dr. Fritz Stiedry was the
conductor, Professor Turnau of the State Opera the
producer, and Professor Eugen Steinhof the stage-
manager. One could see that the effect of this dramatic
experiment—one cannot call it opera—was astoundingly
great. One certainly noticed the difference between the
slight scenic idea and the mastercraft displayed in the
music. It showed, however, such great art that all
hearers were won to the work and Schönberg received
rapturous ovations. Differing from the *Erwartung*, the
style of the *Glückliche Hand* is essentially simple and
clearly formed. The choruses at the beginning and the
end form a frame for the real work, which can be called
an essentially "psychological pantomime," symbolic in
aim. Each scene has its own colour and its own instrumentation, and although the whole work only takes
twenty-three minutes, it is indeed a stirring scene of
plastic expression.

Of one thing one may be certain from a glance at the
score, viz. that the *Glückliche Hand* represents an entirely unheard-of, daring and novel solution to the
problem of scenery; and that in this work a musical
and dramatic style has been created which, if were
rightly understood and correspondingly carried out,
would have as overwhelming an effect as a drama of
Strindberg. For one perceives that it is not a question
of breathing a certain amount of dramatic breath into
people, but rather a highly personal form of expression
through the means of the drama.

K

Schönberg maintained the same style that he had created in *Erwartung* and the *Glückliche Hand*, also in the works that follow, namely *Herzgewächse*, *Pierrot Lunaire* and the *Vier Orchesterlieder*.

HERZGEWÄCHSE

The *Herzgewächse*, Op. 20 (based on a poem by Maurice Maeterlinck), are for high coloratura-soprano, celesta, harmonium, and harp. The voice rises to a high F and in consequence requires as a singer one who can sing the "Queen of the Night" in the *Magic Flute* or "Zerbinetta" in *Ariadne auf Naxos*. The peculiar orchestration makes an exquisite combination of tone-colour possible. I should like to recommend a study of these songs as an introduction to the later works of Schönberg.

PIERROT LUNAIRE

The chief work among this group of songs, however, consists of the *Dreimal sieben Gedichte* (*Thrice Seven Songs*), from Albert Giraud's *Pierrot Lunaire* (German text by Otto Erich Hartleben), which are written for a *Sprechgesang* (song-speech), piano, flute (including piccolo), clarinet (including bass-clarinet), violin (including viola), and violoncello, Op. 21. Schönberg selected these twenty-one songs out of a quantity, the number "three times seven" turning out quite by accident.

Concerning the part of the speaking voice, which in the first performances was undertaken by Frau

Albertine Zehme, Schönberg makes the following announcement in the preface to the work; and this is also of importance for the performance of the part of the speaker in the *Gurre-Lieder*, and of the speaking chorus in the *Glückliche Hand*, in so far as actual singing is not demanded of the latter:

The melody indicated for the speaking voice by notes (apart from a few specially indicated exceptions) is not meant to be sung. The reciter has the task of transforming this melody, always with a due regard to the prescribed intervals, into a speaking melody. That is accomplished in the following way:

1. The rhythm must be kept absolutely strict, as if the reciter were singing; that is to say, with no more freedom than he would allow himself if he were just singing the melody.

2. To emphasise fully the contrast between the sung note and the spoken note, whereas the sung note *preserves* the pitch, the spoken note gives it at first, but abandons it either by rising or by falling immediately after. The reciter must take the greatest care not to fall into a sing-song form of speaking voice; such is absolutely not intended. On the contrary, the difference between ordinary speech and a manner of speech that may be embodied in musical form, is to be clearly maintained. But, again, it must not be reminiscent of song.

This cycle of melodramas consists of three parts, each part containing seven poems. Every poem is differently orchestrated; even when all instruments are employed in the course of the poem, care is taken that in their successive entries each has something characteristic. Thus, for instance, the first of the melodramas, *Mondestrunken (Moonstruck)*, for flute, violin and piano, the 'cello entering later; the second, *Colombine*, for violin and piano, with flute and clarinet in A entering later; the third, *Der Dandy*, for piccolo, clarinet in A and piano; the fourth, *Eine blasse Wäscherin* (*A pale Washerwoman*), for flute, clarinet in A and violin (without piano); the fifth, *Valse de Chopin*, for flute, clarinet in A (later bass-clarinet) and piano; the sixth, *Madonna*, for flute, bass-clarinet and violoncello (piano entering later); the seventh, *Der kranke Mond* (*The Sick Moon*), for flute alone.

In the second part the structural forms begin to predominate, forms which Schönberg here employs with sovereign art. The eighth piece, *Nacht* (*Night*), is a strictly consistent *passacaglia*; the conclusion of the thirteenth, the *Enthauptung* (*Decapitation*), takes up the melody of the solo flute from the *Kranke Mond*, and adds the melody of the spoken song as a part for the bass-clarinet and later for the violoncello, the viola continuing an imitation. The seventeenth, *Parodie*, combines the melody of the viola in imitation, with the melody of the spoken song played by the clarinet in canon. Later a double inverted canon at the half-bar is developed between the recitation and the piccolo in the higher register, and between the clarinet and viola, likewise in inverted canon at the half-bar, while the piano has, as it were, an improvised accompaniment.

The eighteenth, *Der Mondfleck* (*The Moon-spot*), introduces a double canon *cancrizans*, between piccolo and clarinet on the one hand, and violin and 'cello on the other: that is to say, from the middle of the tenth bar onwards, the whole music runs backwards to the beginning. This will be more easy to understand, and some idea will be gathered of the nature of the music, if one looks at the facsimile of a page in the score of *Pierrot Lunaire,* the example being the ninth to the twelfth bars of *Mondfleck* (see below).

In the middle of the second bar, there is a change in the canon just after the word *richtig.* The piccolo plays A flat and then returns to A natural; then follow the notes F, B, C sharp, G, E flat, which appear in the first half of the bar in the contrary order; the same now happens in all the other parts. One can also see that between piccolo and clarinet the canon is at the distance of a quarter-bar, while, between violin and 'cello, it is at the distance of a whole bar. It should also be noticed that at the beginning of the piece, the piccolo and the clarinet carry on the canon in inverted order, the clarinet preceding and the piccolo imitating; whereas, through the abridgment of the cadence, the contrary relation obtains, as a result of the retrogressive movement in the music.

In addition to this double canon, the piano brings in a three-part fugue, the theme of which is the augmentation of the theme of the canon between piccolo and clarinet (in notes of double value), but it does not take part in the retrogressive movement. Throughout the piece, two forms are in evidence: a retrogressive and a progressive form of art in the style of the old masters, especially of the *Kunst der Fuge* (*Art of Fugue*) of J. S. Bach; the like of which in the whole range of modern music I have nowhere found to place beside it. Nevertheless, this extremely intricate construction is not an end in itself, but is cor litioned by the text: "Einen weissen Fleck des hellen M des auf dem Rücken seines schwarzen Rockes, so spaz t Pierrot im lauen Abend" ("With a white spot of the brig t noon falling on the back of his black coat—thus Pie rot makes his promenade in the cool evening").

The melodrama immediately following—*Serenade*, for violoncello and piano—is a long-drawn out, slow, and almost monotonous waltz. The 'cello part here is of such *virtuoso* character that this piece is also played as a concert piece without the reciting voice. The next, *Heimfahrt* (*The Homeward Journey*), is a barcarole with recurring appearances of the various instruments; the last, the epilogue, *O alter Duft aus Märchenzeit* (*O ancient charm of fairy days*), a dreamy, tender, and thoroughly simple song, has the effect of a free improvisation.

. . . .

In *Pierrot Lunaire*, Schönberg created a work which in regard to music, form and content gave ultimate expression to a problem that was already in the air. Schönberg has drawn his *Pierrot* with greater strength and individuality than Stravinsky his *Petrushka*, and has caught each of his moods with unsurpassed skill. That *Pierrot* was a masterpiece was the feeling of all those who heard the work at its first performance; and the feeling was so strong that, despite its daring and novelty, it did not suffer the fate of most of Schönberg's compositions. It was immediately taken up, partly out of respect and partly out of real interest, but in any case with the attention it deserved. In recent years this piece of Schönberg's was studied by Erika Wagner and an ensemble-party, with which Schönberg toured Switzerland and Holland. There followed performances in Paris with Darius Milhaud and Marya Freund, in Copenhagen with Paul v. Klenau and Frau Gutheil-Schoder. To-day *Pierrot Lunaire* is of all the works of Schönberg the best known abroad.

The Four Songs with Orchestra

The first of the *Vier Orchesterlieder* is *Seraphita*, by
Ernest Dowson (the German by Stefan George). It is
written for twenty-four violins, twelve violoncelli, nine
double-basses, six clarinets, one trumpet, three trombones, one bass-tuba, kettle-drums, cymbals, xylophone,
and gong. The violins are divided into six and the 'celli
into three. It begins with an expressive *cantilena* played
by six unison clarinets and accompanied by 'celli divided
in six, and it develops according to certain principles, in
which one can recognise the birth of a new problem
in regard to cadence. The next section, in freer form,
consists of passages for violins, trombones, 'celli and
clarinets, and they prepare for the entry of the voice,
which, indeed, is the chief part: all other themes,
figures, and passages are only of secondary importance.
We quote a passage from the middle of the song, which
is thoroughly characteristic of the style of the *Vier
Orchesterlieder*:

The second song, *Alle, welche dich suchen* (*All that
seek thee*), from the *Stundenbuch* by Rilke, is differently
orchestrated: four flutes, English horn, one clarinet in
D, two clarinets in A, two bass-clarinets, one double-

ʋassoon, one harp, three solo violoncelli, and one solo double-bass. This song is one of very gentle and peaceful mood, the accompaniment being simple but full of expressive warmth.

The third song, *Mach' mich zum Wächter deiner Weiten* (*Make me thy guardian*), also taken from the *Stundenbuch*, is scored for two piccolos, three flutes, three oboes, two English horns, three bass-clarinets, one double-bass clarinet, four solo violins, five solo violoncelli, and one solo double-bass. It is the most polyphonic piece of the group, and with its quite peculiar setting it is certain to call forth entirely unusual and surprising tonal effects.

It is only the fourth song, *Vorgefühl* (*Premonition*), from the *Buch der Bilder* (*Picture Book*) by Rilke, that approximates more or less to the usual orchestral setting. It is scored for one piccolo, three flutes, three oboes, one English horn, three clarinets, one bass-clarinet, three bassoons, one double-bassoon, four horns, one trumpet, one bass-tuba and string quintet. But here also the method of using the various groups of instruments and the combinations of chords is entirely new.

•   •   •   •   •   •

What one learns from the latest of Schönberg's scores is that the possibilities of the modern orchestra are not entirely exhausted, as some musicians, who can go no further, assert. On the contrary, here a beginning, a new way, is pointed out, which shows how the instruments may be used with greater effect than has hitherto been the case: how the setting of chords for solo instruments gives rise to novel and unsuspected combinations of tone. Of course, something more than a mere knowledge of the instruments is required for this kind of orchestration. Indeed, the orchestration begins with the composition itself; for the idea itself is, in the higher sense of the word, *orchestral*, and is not merely orchestrated *afterwards*.

The *Orchesterlieder* were composed in the years 1913–14. Then followed a pause of many years, during which no new works appeared. This silence puzzled many of his friends and followers, who did not perceive that Schönberg was continually working, though no results might be apparent. Of *Die Jakobsleiter* (*Jacob's Ladder*), the poem only has been published, there being only some sketches for the music, though these are already extensive. Since in this oratorio, which is the most comprehensive work that Schönberg has written since the *Gurre-Lieder*, the problems have been transferred from the sphere of the subjective to the cosmic, it may be readily assumed that the music also will be of a different order, and that it will represent another new step in advance.

External circumstances, such as frequently affected Schönberg's life, have up to the present hindered the completion of *Die Jakobsleiter*. But, just as Schönberg renewed his labours on the *Gurre-Lieder* and on the *Glückliche Hand* after a long interruption, one may in this case hope for the completion of the work that is of such importance for his creative activity.

It often happens in the life of men of great moment that Nature herself calls for a halt before new and decisive work is to result. She at the same time demands a certain length of time for the accumulation of strength to create anew. During this time the spirit is not entirely quiescent, but seeks diversion in other forms of activity. Thus it may be explained that Schönberg, after the stormy period of production which lies between 1907 and 1915—during which time he wrote poems, taught and painted—found some years necessary for inner concentration, in order to get a "distant" view both of himself and of his creative work.

LATER WORKS

With the year 1920, an entirely new period of creation began with Schönberg. This period rises to the greatest interest in 1923. To it belong two sets of pianoforte pieces (Op. 23 and 25, both published by Wilhelm Hansen, Copenhagen), the *Serenade* for septet of instruments (and bass-baritone voice in fourth movement only), and the wind quintet. These works did not originate from one another, but stand independently. The first and second of the *Five Piano Pieces*, and a single movement of the *Serenade*, go back to 1920, and the last movement belongs to 1923; whereas the wind quintet belongs to the years 1923 and 1924. In them are included new compositions to which Schönberg has given the title *das Komponieren mit den 12 Tonen*, whose principles are revealed in a series of note-circles. The *Dance Suite for Piano*, Op. 25, consists of six pieces: *Präludium, Gavotte, Musette, Intermezzo, Menuett,* and *Gigue.* They all rest on the same three ground-figures made by four notes, which taken altogether produce the twelve-tone (dodecuple) scale — E-F-G-D flat, G flat-E flat-A flat-D, and B (H in German)-C-A-B flat. From them are derived the inverted formulæ, B-A-G-D flat, A flat-C flat-G flat-C, E flat-D-F-E. Two *Cancrizans* are formed by taking the notes back-

wards. With the third ground-figure the letters B A C H
are produced. In addition, the ground-figure and its
transformations appear in a·quasi-dominant form on
the "diminished fifth," the centre of the dodecuple
scale. All the melodic and harmonic events, which
appear in these six pieces, arise out of the actual
twenty-four forms already derived. The separate four-
note motives appear sometimes melodically as a succession of notes, sometimes as two two-part chords, occasionally as what, on the piano, would be a comfortable
arpeggio stretch of three notes with an added grace-
note before or after; and actual four-part chords made
from them are not rare.

This music is so constructed that it strikes even the
eye by its vivid expression. At the first two private
productions of the *Serenade*, Op. 24, at Dr. Norbert
Schwarzmann's house in Vienna, before a select audience
of over two hundred, and then publicly at the Donaue-
schingen Festival in 1924, this happy handling of new
rules, after the manner of the fugal ones of the old
masters, was received with enthusiasm.

This *Serenade* is written for a combination of clarinet,
bass-clarinet, mandoline, guitar, violin, viola and 'cello,
with a bass-baritone voice for the fourth movement
only. The work is notable for its return to the older
classical forms. The movements are arranged thus—
*March, Minuet, Variations, Sonnet, Dance-Scene, Song
without Words* and *Finale*. The *Song without Words*,
with its unrestrained and freely-flowing sentiment, is
one of the surprises of the work. The other is the
optimism which pervades the whole work, bubbling
up into a new element of humour in the *Dance-Scene*
with its charming *Ländler* rhythm. A number of new

signs are used for indicating the manner of performance, for in no other composer's works is the interpreter tied down to so strict an interpretation of the
musical signs. Indeed, the individuality of the per-
former has entirely disappeared. On the other hand,
the demands made on his executive powers are great
indeed.

The instrumentation is amazing in its complete
mastery. The seven instruments are used throughout
in all the movements. The mandoline and the guitar
are frequently employed to replace the percussion
instruments, and they lend a fascinating colour to the
whole work.

The *Five Piano Pieces*, Op. 23, are written in the
freest possible style. For them, the composer has
adopted a system of special signs for light and heavy
beats, for the normal accent, for the *staccato* and for
the upward and downward sprinkling of the chords.
Like all the works of the later period, they are atonal,
and are all in free rhythm, with the exception of the
last which is in waltz time throughout. The pieces are
all quite short. The first is slow; the second, vehement
and fast; the third (the longest), fantastic and slow;
the fourth, gently swinging; and the last is a waltz.
Most of them start very softly and rise to a great climax
near the end, fading away rapidly, however, into almost
inaudible whispers. They are most pianistic and a little
more developed than the piano pieces of Op. 11.
Great attention is paid to clarity and form. The figures
are conventional in shape, if not in harmony. Gone
are the phantasmagoric visions of the early piano and
the five orchestral pieces. Schönberg has entered upon
a new phase.

Two Bach transcriptions remain to be noticed. They were scored at the suggestion of Josef Stransky, the New York Philharmonic Society's conductor,[1] in the summer of 1922. The works chosen were the two Chorale Preludes, *Schmucke dich* and *Komm, Gott, Schöpfer, heiliger Geist* (No. 17 of the *Eighteen Chorale Preludes*). Schönberg treats the text with the greatest possible reverence, making hardly any additions. The orchestra, however, contains some unexpected instruments. It consists of two flutes, two piccolos, two oboes, two English horns, two E flat clarinets, two bass-clarinets, two bassoons, two double-bassoons, four horns, four trumpets, four trombones, tuba, timpani, triangle, glockenspiel, cymbals, two harps, celesta, and strings. These transcriptions were first played in December 1922 in Carnegie Hall, New York.

.   .   .   .   .   .

In an analysis of Schönberg's artistic progress, the year 1920 must be regarded as the beginning of the third period of his creative work. In the first, he carries the melodic-harmonic development of the romantic style to its utmost point. In the second, from Op. 7 to Op. 22, he turns towards the classical forms; and in the third period, from Op. 23, we find him bringing order to the newly-won tone-material and establishing new rules for it. These rules naturally are not acquired in an abstract manner, but are the results of a technique found in various works of the second period— for example, in the *Passacaglia* entitled *Night*, in *Pierrot Lunaire*.

[1] He resigned the conductorship of the Philharmonic Society in 1923, and became conductor of the State Symphony Orchestra in New York.

Schönberg is for ever seeking, for ever changing. Rest for him is stagnation. In whatever he begins, he is always himself, and thus real art is the result. One is reminded of Verlaine's verse:

L'art, mes enfants, c'est d'être absolument soi-même,
Et qui m'aime me suive et qui me suit, qu'il m'aime.

In his later period of composition, Schönberg developed so quickly, that one cannot imagine whither his way will lead. And whereas at first he was quite alone, later gathering about him a small circle of pupils which gradually developed into a growing community, we now see his work meeting with recognition in other countries also; and that artists like Busoni, Ravel, and Stravinsky have shown tendencies approximating to his, all appearing to be striving after some common goal. For each of these artists proceeds according to the laws of his nature, and according to his own creative experience; yet all are united by the common bond of an inward commandment that bids them forsake the older paths and seek out fresh ones.

During the time in which I was occupied with the preparation and writing of this book, and in which I devoted myself exclusively to Schönberg's music, I formed quite a clear idea of his function as an artist. I felt the steadiness of his development, the rapid course of his path, and I recognised in each one of his works the full measure of his personality. His wonderful command of the means at his disposal permits of his mastering the greatest difficulties. Thus he can apply his undivided power to the development of the *personal* in the truest sense of the word, and to that which is beyond and above tradition and convention.

Whatever be the attitude of later time towards him, it will be impossible to overlook the fact that it was he who broke through accepted musical conventions which threatened to become mere externalities; that he sacrificed himself, and, by traversing the road of suffering, along which his works stand as visible monuments of the various stages of his painful career, has given to music a new *ethos*, and a sincerity that renounces all that is merely relative and lies outside its own sphere.

It is not the representation of external events as in Naturalism; not the reflection of things that call forth moods within, as in Impressionism; not the persistent manifestation of the *ego*, as in Expressionism, that can be regarded as the essential in his art. The inner significance of his music is not circumscribed by any of these three conceptions of art, which our age so readily adopts as symbolic of a reality that is only apparent.

It contains elements of all of these, but it regulates them according to a formative power which is hidden in the deepest impulses of the creative spirit in music.

The *élan vital* of this music seeks for its laws in the mystical language of a music whose principles we feel before we can express them. It creates for itself the proper form of its inmost springs of life. It rises to the mastery of the word in poetry, and forces poetry into its service. It breathes its own breath into the rhythm of this music and lets the *cæsuræ* fall where the wave of inner feeling, which had borne a musical thought on its crest, begins to ebb away. It enlarges the connections that exist between motive and motive, theme and counter-theme, antecedent and consequent; but it knows, through its supreme mastery, how to preserve them from disintegration.

Thus the great destroyer of old values, apparently the most complex phenomenon that the present time has brought forth, becomes a purifying power, the importance of which contemporary people are scarcely yet in a position to appreciate, but the effect of which they already begin to feel. For Schönberg has swept away all half-measures and half-truths. He has created a standard which is important for the right appreciation of the general *niveau* of music. The pathos of the post-Wagnerian music has lost its power, since he substituted for it a more sustained musical idiom. The brilliance of the Neo-Romantic orchestra seems like false glitter beside the masterly orchestration of his later works, which attempts no longer to give colour to the melodic line, but to give expression to the musical thought in its most intensive form.

Standing on the threshold of two epochs, Schönberg's art has, nevertheless, none of the characteristics of transition; for he does not allow himself to be borne along with the times, but it is he himself who hastens onwards in his epoch-making advance.

Concentration on the strength of his own personality, beginning with the *Klavierstücke*, Op. 11, has allowed him in a few years to proceed along the path of development, for the accomplishment of which one might have supposed that the efforts of generations would have been necessary. And whoever knows Schönberg, knows full well that even his latest achievement marks no conclusion, no halting, but is only another step forwards on the way towards the great transformation to what is higher and purer, in accordance with the words uttered by the archangel Gabriel to the Striving One in his *Jakobsleiter*:

Whether to the right, whether to the left, whether forwards or backwards, whether up hill or down—one must go on without asking what lies before, or what lies behind. It must remain concealed; one must forget it in order to accomplish one's task.

CHRONOLOGICAL TABLE

1897. Pianoforte edition of Zemlinsky's opera *Sarema*.
String Quartet in D major (unpublished).

1898. Two Songs, Op. 1. Dreililien Edition.

1898–1900. Four Songs, Op. 2. Dreililien Edition.
Six Songs, Op. 3. Dreililien Edition.

1899. Sextet, *Verklärte Nacht*, Op. 4. Dreililien Edition.

1900–1901. Composition of the *Gurre-Lieder*, and orchestration of the first and second parts and beginning of the third.
Orchestration of operettas.

1902–1903. *Pelleas und Melisande*, Op. 5. Universal Edition.

1904. Six Songs with Orchestra, Op. 8. Universal Edition.

1904–1905. First String Quartet in D minor, Op. 7. Dreililien Edition.

1905. Eight Songs, Op. 6. Dreililien Edition.

1906. Chamber-Symphony in E major, Op. 9. Universal Edition.

1906–1907. Two Ballades, Op. 12. Universal Edition.

1907. *Friede auf Erden*, Op. 13. Tischer und Jagenberg.
Two Songs, Op. 14. Universal Edition.

1907–1908. Second String Quartet in F sharp minor, Op. 10. Universal Edition.

1908. Fifteen Songs from Stefan George's *Das Buch der hängenden Gärten*, Op. 15. Universal Edition.

1909. Three Piano Pieces, Op. 11. Universal Edition.
Five Orchestral Pieces, Op. 16. C. F. Peters.
Erwartung, Op. 17. Universal Edition.
Article "On Music Criticism," in *Der Merker*, I. 2.

1910–1911. *Harmonielehre.* Manual of Harmony. Universal Edition.

Orchestration of the third part of the *Gurre-Lieder.* Universal Edition.

1910–1913. *Die glückliche Hand,* Op. 18, words and music. Universal Edition.

1911. Six Short Piano Pieces, Op. 19. Universal Edition.

Herzgewächse, Op. 20. Universal Edition.

In Memory of Gustav Mahler, in *Der Merker,* III. 5.

Problems of the Teaching of Art. In the *Musikalisches Taschenbuch,* Vienna.

1912. *Pierrot Lunaire,* Op. 21. Universal Edition.

Orchestration of Löwe's *Der Nöck* (Universal Edition); of Beethoven's *Adelaide;* and several of Schubert's songs (unpublished).

Speech in Memory of Gustav Mahler.

Parsifal und Urheberrecht (Parsifal and Copyright). In the *Konzert-Taschenbuch,* Vienna.

1913–1914. Four Songs with Orchestra, Op. 22. Universal Edition.

1915. Poem of the *Totentanz der Prinzipien* (unpublished).

Poem of the oratorio *Die Jakobsleiter.* Universal Edition.

1915–1917. Composition of *Die Jakobsleiter* (unfinished).

1920–1923. Five Piano Pieces, Op. 23 (published by Hansen, Copenhagen).

1921–1923. *Serenade,* Op. 24, for clarinet, bass-clarinet, mandoline, guitar, violin, viola, 'cello, and a bass-baritone voice (Hansen).

1923. Dance Suite for Piano (Hansen).

1923–1924. Wind Quintet, Op. 26 (Universal Edition).

The works appearing in the Dreililien Edition have now been taken over by the Universal Edition, Vienna.

INDEX

Figures in heavy type refer to pages on which works are discussed in detail, with musical illustrations.